The Seven Laws of Money

THE
SEVEN LAWS
OF MONEY

Michael Phillips

SHAMBHALA

Boston & London

1993

Shambhala Publications, Inc.
Horticultural Hall
300 Massachusetts Avenue
Boston, Massachusetts 02115

9 8 7 6 5 4 3 2

Printed in China on acid-free paper ⊗
Distributed in the United States
by Random House, Inc., and in Canada by
Random House of Canada Ltd
See page 197 for Library of Congress
Cataloging-in-Publication Data.

CONTENTS

The Seven Laws of Money

——— THE FIRST LAW ———

DO IT!

*Money Will Come When You Are
Doing the Right Thing*

THE FIRST LAW is the hardest for most people to accept and is the source of the most distress.

The clearest translation of this in terms of personal advice is "go ahead and do what you want to do." Worry about your ability to do it and your competence to do it but certainly do not worry about the money.

Let me give you a number of examples from my own personal experience where this sort of advice was extremely successful. The Book Fair, The First International San Francisco Book Fair, was being organized, and at the first meeting we became bogged down in the issue of how much to charge and whether the fees we could collect would be enough to cover the cost of the exhibition hall and other expenses. This was a situation where extraordinary people were working together with outstanding ideas and an enormous amount of energy, and they had rapidly become bogged down in the potential agonies of how to plan for money. Fortunately, I was able to say "Don't anybody worry about the money; I'll worry about it." Everybody just looked at me as I said that, and based on my background they accepted it. From that point on money was not discussed by the group except in a very perfunctory way, and as the energies were channeled into the appropriate directions the Book Fair became an outstanding success. At no time either before or during the event was money a problem, as I knew full well would be the case.

Since this was an extraordinarily good idea the money just came in. Just rolled in. There was more than enough to pay for everything that was needed.

I have gone to many meetings, listened to many discussions and watched many groups form, start to think about money, start to plan for money, set out to raise the money and then cease to exist. That seems to be the crux of many ventures. They rapidly get bogged down in money and neglect the project and their own personal goals.

I was advising Salli Rasberry on starting a free school. I pointed out that at the first meeting the people involved should deliberately avoid the subject of money, since if they were to discuss how much it would cost to hire teachers, what buildings would cost, etc. their project would likely be doomed at the outset. I suggested that the rules should be interpreted as "do it" and the money would follow. A way to avoid the problem of the first meeting and the general concern about money would be to designate one person or a group of people to worry about money so that other peoples' energies would not become diverted.

Once two men who were planning to start an organization with an interesting idea came to me. They wanted some money to buy a building. I told them that before taking steps to buy a building they needed thirty people or so to sign a piece of paper saying that they were also interested in the organization. By the time the two men came back they had over 250 members in their organization. It had grown to astronomic size in six months. Every once in a while they came back to talk about money. The fact is, with that kind of membership and that kind of energy they have more than adequate resources at their disposal to accomplish anything the group wishes to do, and money is secondary.

The examples I have given have been taken from my role as a consultant in helping groups get started by taking their minds off money. The essential argument, plea, advice here is that if an idea is good enough, and the people involved want it badly enough, they'll begin to put their own personal energy and time into it, and the idea will soon be its own reward. Money itself cannot accomplish their goal; only the people themselves can accomplish it. Maybe that's an abstract interpretation of the law, but it's certainly the result of a great deal of experience. Of the people I have explained this concept to, only a rare few have been able to understand that if they work hard enough on their project money would follow.

Often people say to me "What am I going to do next month? How am I to live until I get this thing started?" What I try to tell them is to get started; go forward;

get something done. You have to worry about money for the next month as your own personal problem, in any case. Try to separate the issue of the project you're working on from your own problem of survival. If you're going to predicate the project's survival on your own need to be comfortable for the coming month, you have already doomed the project. Figure out how you're personally going to survive and then, separately, how important the project is to you. You're going to have to continue to support yourself anyway, and when you're working on the project that's an added burden. But the project per se, the success of the project per se, will be seriously jeopardized if you integrate your own need to make a living with the needs of the project.

One of my friends, upon hearing this advice, decided that his particular project was so important to him, and he felt that he could make enough progress on it in two months, that he sold all the books he owned and lived off the revenue for two months. As of now, he has no qualms about that decision. The project was a more than adequate reward.

COMMENTARY ON
THE FIRST LAW OF MONEY

Money, which represents the prose of life, and which is hardly spoken of in parlors without an apology, is in its effects and laws, as beautiful as roses.

—RALPH WALDO EMERSON,
Nominalist and Realist

The most difficult thing for people to understand about money is that money will come to you if you are doing the right thing. Money is secondary to what you are doing.

Most of this chapter deals with that statement. I have said it time and again and am always amazed to find that people cannot accept it. Most people can't accept it even when it comes from their own experience. Yet I keep getting more and more evidence to support it and virtually no signs to indicate the opposite.

Many people have argued that what I say is a self-fulfilling prophecy. They say that I can claim that if a project fails or if somebody doesn't get money when they seem to be doing a good job they aren't doing the right thing. Indeed, taken at face value, there is a logical fallacy to this first law. Many people prefer to deal with the logical fallacy of it instead of dealing with its reality.

There are logical fallacies in all the Seven Laws. They cannot be arrived at by a "logical" process. The Seven Laws deal with a part of man that is outside the realm of the typical body of Western thought. You logicians out there will recognize what I mean when I say that it is to be found in Wittgenstein's *Tractus Logicus*; theologians will recognize it by the phrase "transcendental."

The realm of logic in Western man comprises about 2% of his reality. The remaining 98% of reality includes feelings, sex, art, non-verbal communication, most of our sensual inputs, etc. The Seven Laws deal with the operating relationships that exist in the 98% of the world where our logic doesn't apply.

Let me use the example of tariffs to illustrate the divergence between logic as it is used by man and the way the world operates. Ever since the 18th Century, when Adam Smith first began studying economics, it has been very apparent that international tariffs and quotas that exist between countries are not rational or logical. Significantly better arguments can be made for free trade than can ever be made for tariffs. Just briefly, if you are not an economist, the two classical arguments *for* tariffs were "protection of infant industries" and "domestic defense."

An example of what "protection of infant industries" covers is as follows: Let's assume that you want to start a small business. You have discovered that your new business can be carried on profitably. The problem is, though, that the initial cost of *getting into* the business is too great and the prices of your first products would have to be very high. Because they were so high people would continue to buy cheaper products from other countries.

If you rely on logic, the answer to this classic dilemma would not be to impose tariffs but to provide a direct government subsidy to help you start your business.

The argument in favor of "domestic defense" is that we must have our own home oil industries, for example, so that we don't have to rely on other countries in war time. There is a comparable *logical* answer, however, that rules out the need for tariffs.

Throughout history, however, even since Adam Smith and his followers made their rational, clear arguments *for* free trade, we have always had tariffs. During this time there have been enlightened kings, enlightened presidents, and enlightened councils of economic advisors, all fully understanding the logical arguments—yet tariffs have not given way to free trade. To me this is proof that there is something significantly more powerful than logic operating in international economic relations, something that we don't understand. Hopefully, our rationale and our logic will catch up with the facts of reality. All of which leads me back to the First Law of Money and the logical fallacy of it, which is that attempting to understand the law by trying to think about it is not going to be much help. In many ways it is like trying to understand Zen Buddhism through logic rather than feeling. You cannot talk about an experience and expect another person to substitute your words for his lack of experience.

The concept that money "will come to you" is clearly very mystical. Sometimes when one tries to bring something mystical into his daily life the conflict with the world of logic can lead to unusual results.

Several months ago, in offering advice on money, I ran into trouble by using mystical premises. A good friend of mine in the foundation business was planning to leave the country. He had a commitment to a friend of his, a famous lawyer, to raise enough money so that the lawyer could travel and study in Europe for nine months. My friend cajoled me into accepting responsibility for raising the $8,000 needed. The reason he wanted someone to take this responsibility was to enable the lawyer to continue to work on an important lawsuit and not be diverted by worrying about money.

I met the lawyer and made it clear to him that I would accept the responsibility; first, however, I had a nominal number of things for him to do. The actual words I used were "I will accept the responsibility for seeing that you get the money. I don't guarantee with absolute certainty that you'll get the amount you want, but you should go ahead and do exactly what you're supposed to do and plan the trip on the assumption that you will have the money." That was it. On two occasions, after I had done some investigation, I asked him to write letters. At one point I wrote him a letter suggesting he do two specific things.

About six weeks before his trip was to begin he phoned in the evening and insulted me in the most incredible terms I had heard in years. The gist of his fury was that although I had said I would help him raise the money, I had done nothing at all, while he had spent an enormous amount of time and had worried endlessly trying to raise the money. After he had calmed down a little, I found out that he had not done most of the things I had asked him to do because he had doubted my ability to raise money. It turned out that he was willing to call and berate me because he had *gotten* a grant. As the reader may have guessed, the grant had come from one of the first people I had told him to send a letter to.

I was sorry about the whole matter. The lawyer operated in a very logical and goal-oriented world, highly planned in monetary terms, expecting me to do a lot of running around, while I had operated on my mystical premise in accepting this particular responsibility.

This is an example both of how the First Law works and of how recommending that someone else operate on the basis of the First Law can lose you a few friends. People who have strong, money-oriented goals are not going to accept this almost mystical view. If you are as foolish as I was, and try to be an intermediary between their goals and some other responsibility you may lose a friend too.

You may be reading this book from the perspective of a person trying to carry out a project to build a windmill or a diving bell, or trying to figure out how to get to the Middle East so you can walk to Mecca on your knees. On the other hand, you may be reading simply because you want to know "How do I get a job? How do I save up enough money to buy a car, pay the bills, and get enough money to buy some milk for the baby?" There is, in my mind, a distinction between these, and the separation occurs when the project is different from and independent of you, when it is distinct in your own mind from what you consider to be a "living." To take the example of the diving bell: if the diving bell is for pleasure or for looking at fish, it is part of a project; on the other hand, if you are an ichthyologist who makes his living photographing fish and writing about them, then the diving bell is part of your livelihood. My advice is that you should recognize that you are always going to have to eat, that you are going to have to survive the next week, month, or hour, and that you should distinguish the priority of the project from your day-to-day work. Unfortunately, many people can't separate the two, and the net result is that their belief that the project they are working on is the most important thing they can do gets coupled with their conviction that they have to survive. The combination of these two ideas leads them to believe that *the world owes them a living.*

I question whether mankind has reached the stage where we can view everyone as deserving financial support for his lifetime. Our current view is that children, the mentally retarded and senile, as well as the physically ill and disabled, are entitled to support. Whether in time that will expand to include more people, I don't know. At the present time, in your own particular case, I think it is best to consider whether you are capable both of providing for yourself and doing your project too.

The matter is quite different when your livelihood and your desired activities are integrated; this is where the concept of right livelihood enters. Right livelihood is something I learned from Dick Baker, a Zen Buddhist roshi. I don't know its origins, and I'm not certain of its history. I can't tell you directly whether you are involved in right livelihood. However, I can suggest some of the questions you might ask yourself. Please don't take me too literally—this is not a typical *Cosmopolitan* questionnaire to measure something like whether you are gay or straight.

It is simply a way to give you a perspective on what right livelihood is.

First of all, do you think you can undertake your work for a long time? Right livelihood could be spending a whole life as a carpenter, for example. One of the qualities of right livelihood is that within it, within the practice of it, is the perfection of skills and qualities that will give you a view of the universe. Constant perfection or practice of a right livelihood will give you a view of the whole world, in a sense similar to Hemingway's story of *The Old Man and the Sea*. In Hemingway's story the old man's life as a fisherman gives him a connection with the entire world, and a "whole world of experience." What are the rewards? Right livelihood has within itself its own rewards; it deepens the person who practices it. When he is twenty years old he is a little different from the person he will be at thirty, and he will be even more different when he's forty, and fifty. Aging works *for* you in right livelihood. It's like a good pipe or a fine violin; the more you use it the deeper its finish.

Another thing you can ask yourself about right livelihood is whether the good intrinsic in your livelihood is also good in terms of the greater community. This is a hard question to answer when you are asking it about yourself. It's hard to establish criteria, but a carpenter can certainly be doing good for the community in a very powerful sense. All of this is by way of saying that you shouldn't separate the idea of doing good from whatever your livelihood is; they can be integrated. With a right livelihood you would not be doing what you are doing and at the same time be saying "I'd rather be a nurse, I would rather be head of the Red Cross." The dichotomy would not be necessary. What you would be doing, in your eyes, would be as beneficial to the community as any other function.

I have tried to give a few guidelines on right livelihood. However, experience is a part of livelihood that cannot be described in words. The words and phrases I use are necessarily trivial descriptions, such as your job and you are "centered," or the relationship between who you are and what you do is "focused." These are cliche, and they miss the point. But they give you a hint in the same sense that stained glass windows give you a hint of a rainbow.

Right livelihood is a concept that places money secondary to what you are doing. It's something like a steam engine, where the engine, fire and water working together create steam for forward motion. Money is like steam; it comes from the interaction of fire (passion) and water (persistence) brought together in the right circumstance, the engine.

The concept of money as something of secondary importance if you are doing the right thing has not been difficult for me to accept. A good example comes from my personal life.

In my late teens I tried to decide whether to be an artist or to follow another career. I asked one of my mother's friends, a very respected and well-known sculptor, to look at my paintings and tell me whether I could be an artist. What he said when he looked at them was: "They are very nice. Whether you are an artist or not is not visible. It depends on whether you can work eight hours a day every day." It happens that he was a Japanese sculptor, maybe with a touch of Zen training.

I know that if I were to work eight hours a day at my art, within four or five years I would be able to make a living at it. With that much time, energy, devotion and self-focusing, what I am would emerge in my art sufficiently to be recognized as having value. I don't see that as different from a man who goes into the business world or who works in his grocery store eight hours a day. He certainly has to expect to work at what he is doing, to develop his skills and to make a living at it, and he can't expect it to take much less than five years.

If you are devoted enough and can find enough passion within yourself, you will find an almost infinite number of ways to make a living at the things you want to do. The way this book is being done is an example; it embodies my advice to artists—the hardest group for me to deal with in explaining the First Law.

If an artist recognizes that reaching financial success is mostly a matter of fate rather than a matter of talent, and he can find other people who agree with him, he has tremendous leverage. What can be done then is powerful. A group of relatively unknown artists who consider themselves peers can form a small non-profit institution. Within five years it is almost a certainty that, if they indeed form a pool of talent better than the average, money will flow in. Maybe the group has the talents of the Rod McKuen, Jonathan Livingston Seagull type; maybe their talents are more similar to Hemingway's or T. S. Eliot's. In either case, within five years that group is going to see revenue coming in, and probably they can all live on it.

Aside from furnishing a source of income, there are two advantages to this kind of group. The first is a recognition that selection by the economic forces of the market place is not necessarily a recognition of innate talent. The second is that the reward of money from the market place should not be taken as a key as to how the artist should develop his skills. There have been many fine artists who were rewarded monetarily when they were still relatively young and who subsequently did not develop much beyond that point (Dali, Stravinsky, Hans Hoffman). They continued to produce what they were most rewarded for, and their art, or their talent, became stereotyped and did not progress. In many ways this can be avoided by a cooperative group effort because the individual can continue to produce what he is best capable of. If he is on his own and he gets rewarded by ten, fifty or a hundred thousand dollars from the sale of a work of art, it is almost inevitable that his next work of art is going to be very similar, and so on and so on as the rewards come in.

There's an interesting connection I'd like to point out between doing "the right thing" and getting a bank loan. Banks are highly mysterious organizations to just about everybody, including bankers. (The mystery helps to cover up the difference between the good bankers and the bad ones.) I have a number of private business clients right now, and I often take them to the bank to get loans. One of the things that I have found about a good banker is that he does not make purely rational judgments. He does expect each client to have loan papers and related material in good order—not because the papers or the numbers on them have particular magical significance but because the client's ability to perceive the importance of these papers are all reflections on himself. A good bank loan officer will always say that he makes his loan decision on the "quality" of the borrower. A "quality" borrower is one who is wholly integrated into the function for which he is seeking a loan and is perfectly capable of what he has set out to do. I make sure myself that my client has these qualities before I send him into a bank. (Banks are cold and austere, and many of the loan officers I've known have been grumpy, nasty, insensitive people. Only a few of them are able to understand, sympathize and intuitively evaluate the potential borrower as a person.) A client will be judged on whether or not the business is meeting the needs of its community—because if it is it will be rewarded with profits.

I fear that I may have misled a few readers with some of my examples. I can see where someone might say, "Well, I'll drop some acid, snort a lot of coke and get on with my thing and not worry about money." I can also hear some other readers saying, "First I've got to sit and meditate on what the right thing is, and second get things going smoothly around here so that everything is running perfectly. Then third, I want this house spotless, and fourth, I want everybody to be spiffy and well-dressed. Then the money will just come driving up the turnpike when everything is looking cool and clean."

Now maybe these two approaches will

work, but what I am driving at is a little different. My authority does not come from a rational point of view, and I could be wrong, so I certainly hope nobody reading this book takes it as gospel. My understanding of the First Law of Money is that a person's focus must be on his passion. He must be able to integrate who he is with what he is doing, see his project as a whole, and do his work systematically in order to legitimately expect the money to take on its secondary "helping" role.

The analogy that comes to mind when I think of this middle ground between avoiding money and focusing on it is the eye. In order for you to see, your eye cannot be perfectly still. The eye itself vibrates. If it stops or is held it overloads, and there is no image either. For the image to appear you need some combination of stability and movement. The same applies to money.

There is something else I want to discuss under the First Law—the life cycle and money. It is helpful to remember that once we were all children, unable to support ourselves, and that at some point again before our deaths most of us will be physically unable to provide a living for ourselves. In between these periods, the issue of providing sustenance for ourselves and others becomes an issue. It is interesting that in most cultures there are periods of apprenticeship and low wages, and there is a period of increasing wages prior to retirement. In the United States, if one looks at a simple chart of income distribution it is very skewed; it looks unfair because the 20% of the population which has the highest wages earns more than 80% of the income. However, when one looks at the distribution in terms of life cycle, comparing people in their twenties to those in their fifties and correcting for the fact that over their work-life the income of the younger ones significantly increases, then the unfairness (inequality of income) seems almost to disappear.

In your own life there should be some recognition that you are probably going to live quite a while. You can change your horizons when you realize this. You will have fewer immediate desires and probably a greater potential to find out what you want to do. As you get older your ability to survive and your rapport with other people will undoubtedly be a reflection of your comfort with yourself and your awareness of who you are. All of which suggests that it makes sense to think in a fairly broad perspective and to realize that when you are young it is very unlikely that you are going to have a substantial amount of money unless you inherit it, and that then is the time to accept your status, develop your skills, potentials and qualities. It's summed up in a phrase that Portola Institute developed: "A willingness to fail young."

Sometimes people come to me with the knowledge that I am going to advise them to go ahead and do what they do best, and the money will come. There seem to be three different reasons why they ask for my advice:

1. There are some who want to hear it from me personally so they can accept it for reasons of authority.
2. Some think that accepting it will lead to direct results, that maybe because I am a foundation man I will be so impressed with their hard work that I will give them a grant.
3. Finally, there are some who don't really know it but *think* they do—and want endorsement.

In the latter case I am reminded of a story about a psychologist who used a test on business executives to determine how successful they might turn out to be. One of the pictures he used in the test depicted a man on a rope, which he would ask the executives to describe. If the executive described the man as climbing the rope, he was judged to be aggressive and successful. If the man on the rope was described as simply hanging on, the executive was judged to be a man who was interested primarily in trying to maintain his job and who thus wouldn't get very far in the company. If the executive described the man on the rope as climbing down, he had really made up his mind to quit the company, or to retire.

An article about the test and the picture of the man on the rope was published in *Time*. Shortly thereafter, one of the psychologist's patients came in and said he had read the *Time* article and that he knew what the answer should be. "Well, that man is going up," he said. "I know he's supposed to be going up. He's probably going up because there's a lion at the bottom of the rope snapping at his feet."

Clearly, he knew the direction the man should go, but he didn't understand the ideas behind the interpretation of the picture.

MONEY HAS ITS OWN RULES.

Records, Budgets, Saving, Borrowing

THE RULES OF MONEY are probably Ben Franklin-type rules, such as never squander it, don't be a spendthrift, be very careful, you have to account for what you're doing, you must keep track of it, and you can never ignore what happens to money.

The high priests of money, particularly of Law Two, are obviously accountants. Maybe we should have a cult in which accountants are worshipped; projects related to that cult would probably be very successful. Maybe we don't think about the magic and spectacular mysticism implicit in what accountants do. Accountants can handle the books of General Motors in exactly the same way that they can do the most bizarre tattoo parlor, and from their point of view there is little difference. One may be a little more complex than the other but they are done exactly the same way.

What does an accountant do? He looks at what is coming in, he records the sources of income, he sees what records are kept and examines all the details of how monies were expended. He studies the records to see how the money flowed through and where it was stored at any particular time. He uses such things as an income and expense statement or an asset and liability statement. These are simply records of the flow of money kept in accurate detail by general categories. The rule of money is that you just can't hand several people checks and say go ahead, write the checks you want on this checking account; you can't! Someone has to be responsible for knowing what check was written, where it went and where the funds were coming from. Those are the rules of money and they are absolute.

How does this translate into the daily life of operating projects? First, all expenses must be kept track of, *all* expenses, and where a receipt is possible a receipt should be kept. It's possible for you to set some lower limit below which it's not necessary to keep extremely detailed accounts; if you're really poor that might mean keeping careful track of everything over fifty cents. If you're rich you might keep careful track of everything over ten dollars. Once you set this minimum for record keeping you must observe it. If, at any time, you should get lost in your record keeping, say after two months, and you find you're stuck and things don't balance, you have to stop what you're doing, go back, and straighten it out step by step until it is correct.

Most inexperienced people make the mistake of ignoring this essential rule of money, and many sophisticated people do too. I have one client in particular who has a very successful firm. Last year the client was in very serious trouble and invited me in as a consultant. The first thing I did was to have an accountant prepare a careful analysis of the firm's expenses and a month-to-month record over a six month period of what the company had been doing. I also had a careful set of books drawn up for the company. What this client had been doing without being the slightest bit conscious of it was to go deeper and deeper in the hole every month. He wasn't even aware of it. The cash flow was fine, he always seemed to have just enough cash in the bank, he always seemed to be just meeting his payroll and he didn't worry about it. His sales continued to grow. The fact is that when I came in he was in debt on his books by more than $15,000 and getting deeper in debt. Less than a year later that debt had been totally wiped out and the principals were at least $15,000 richer in a visible monetary way. This is not preposterous or an extreme example. It is quite common for businesses to be insensitive to money problems and the requirements of money, assuming that just because it's coming in they are profitable and doing well.

COMMENTARY ON THE SECOND LAW

We can't list the rules of money, unfortunately, because they are more like an ethic than a list. They do not tell you what to do, like an abacus where you add when two beads are down and subtract when three beads are up. The rules tell you that in certain situations, by following a particular line of behavior, there will be certain beneficial consequences, and things will turn out okay in the long run. Like all ethics, the rules operate at many levels. If you fail at one level, they tell you what level to go to next. It's a comprehensive system.

The first and clearest rule is that you have to keep track of your money. You have to know approximately how much you have, how much you are spending, how much is coming in, and what the general direction of your dollar flow is. A good diversion at this point, necessary to help keep track of money, is to have an idea of what in mathematics is called "significant digits." If you didn't learn it in high school, it can be summarized in a few words: any form of measurement has some degree of precision beyond which increased precision is of no use and below which lack of precision makes the entire venture useless.

Let me give you a personal example. My oldest daughter, Cynthia, says it's "about a mile" from my house to my ex-wife Helen's house, where she lives. What she's saying is that it takes approximately five minutes by car, ten to twelve minutes walking. For her, a mile is essentially a rounded-off measure; she talks in terms of half a mile, a mile, one and a half miles, and so on. She's rounding off the distance by approximately half a mile. That is useful in terms of the amount of time and the type of traveling she and I do, since the only two means of travel we use between the two houses are foot and car. If Cynthia were flying over that same distance, however, the distance between the two houses would be so insignificant it would hardly be mentionable. The houses would appear to be right next to each other. If she were pushing a wheelbarrow of heavy stuff, or moving a refrigerator from one house to the other on a dolly, the fact that it is actually 4,800 feet instead of "a mile" would be of some consolation, in the same sense that the front stairway having 20 steps instead of 26 would be of some consolation. On the other hand, if I were laying a wire between the two houses for an intercom it would be very significant for me to know the number of feet within at least fifty feet. (It would be useless for me to know it within a few inches, because there would be at least that much stretch in the wire.) I hope that gives you an idea of what "significant digits" are. They are a measure of precision relative to what you are doing.

In terms of the use of money there is something comparable to "significant digits" when you keep track of expenditures. If you earned $30,000 a year, for example, and had savings of $10,000 it probably wouldn't make any difference if you didn't keep track of the total of one days' expenses when you were shopping in Acapulco. Forgetting about a couple of hundred dollars wouldn't be too serious.

If you had planned in advance that the total week-long trip would cost you, say $1,700, being off by two hundred dollars would just mean taking a little more out of your savings account. However the opposite would be the case if your income were only $7,000 and your savings were small. A misjudgment of two hundred dollars could take you as much as six months to replace in your savings, six months in terms of cutting costs and taking peanut butter and jelly sandwiches for lunch.

There are certain types of work involving precision that deal more with the ethic of money and less with the significant digit aspects. I have to confess that when I was a banker I allowed myself one form of petty larceny: when I went to a business lunch I would include a 35 cent Garcia y Vega cigar on my luncheon tab. Sometimes I even allowed myself two or three, depending upon how many I thought I would smoke that day. The total bill, of course, was picked up by my bank expense account. I could certainly come up with ten or fifteen rationalizations as to why that was perfectly okay, but that's irrelevent. Within the money ethic it is not okay for the banker to perpetrate any form of larceny, even if it amounts to only 35 cents.

In England, what I did is called a "fiddle." British folklore says that every man has his fiddle; it's the tiny bit of cheating he does.

The important point I want to bring out here is that the cheating should be within some controllable emotional limit. When I became treasurer of the Glide Foundation, knowing that I readily had access to several million dollars (to potentially be able to abscond with it), I stopped the cigar bit and made sure that all expense bills were accurate to within 5 cents. When I go out to lunch now I am very careful to make a note of the precise amount, and if I don't remember for sure I underestimate it. There's some danger point that triggers in everybody's mind a feeling of "Well, I've done a little bit; maybe I'll do a little bit more the next time," and you have to know what that trigger point is. With me, when there are several million dollars I could potentially steal, five cents is that trigger point. When I was a banker and could steal very little but *could* abuse an expense account to the tune of two or three thousand dollars a year, 35 cents was the trigger point I allowed myself.

An example of a man who didn't know his trigger point is Fred, an embezzler who was working in the operations department of our bank. When he was finally caught everyone was completely surprised. Fred was a very meek man in his late fifties, shy, quiet, retiring. He was very pleasant. Fred was always given a relatively secure job. We all relied on him to do his work, knowing he wouldn't create trouble and that he'd be around for a long time.

In the early 1950s, when he was a low-level employee, probably a head teller, Fred had begun to make some money on his own in uranium stock, the kind that was being sold out of Salt Lake City. He was so happy and proud of himself that he began telling his friends to buy uranium stock. As the stock rose in value he encouraged more and more of his friends to buy more and more stock. His friends began to see him as some sort of financial genius, and many of them sold their personal belongings, borrowing along with him to invest in uranium stock. However, the uranium bubble soon burst, and nearly everybody involved lost significant amounts of money. Most of Fred's friends set about learning to live with their losses, but Fred felt that their losses were some sort of reflection on him as a person. He became generous with his friends, taking them to lunch, giving them gifts—initially within his salary, within his ability to pay. Before long, though, he began to feel that his gifts were a poor substitute for the losses his friends had suffered. Fred began to embezzle on a small scale—a little bit of cash here, a little bit of cash there.

As his job responsibilities within the bank increased, he progressed to a position where he was in charge of the bank control accounts, one of the core parts of banking. This is the "account" which adjusts the total amount of money that a bank handles every day so that balance sheets come out equal on both sides. Not only was he in charge of this account; he also learned how to embezzle from it.

Over an eight-to-ten-year period he came to realize that nobody could check his system, since he was the only one who fully understood it. Whenever anybody came in to examine the books he was always there. He almost never took a vacation, because he didn't dare teach anybody how to handle the bank control account. He was taking increasingly more money, gambling occasionally to try to win to pay it back but usually using it to buy back worthless uranium stock from his friends.

Fred was caught because he finally went on vacation, and while he was gone someone *had* to figure out his books. It was discovered that he had taken $300,000.

This is what I consider a fairly typical case. I mention it because it deals with the trigger point of emotional control. There is some point for everyone at which they can no longer control themselves.

While we're on the subject of embezzlement I'd like to mention something my mother, who is a radical, used to say: "People who steal bread to feed their families are the ones who go to jail, and people who steal hundreds of millions (in the form of profits) are the ones who succeed." Wonderful as she is, I disagree with her on this. Certainly a high percentage of poor people who steal bread *do* get caught and *do* get punished. However, it doesn't follow that actually stealing *money* on a large scale is unpunishable. The folk phrase she is quoting confuses Marxist views of profit with actual theft. This view is based on the assumption that if someone *else* has more money than you there must be something wrong. He must have gotten it by doing something bad (like stealing). Or, more abstractly, what he did to get it (earn profits) is bad.

In fact, the more money you steal, the more likely you are to get caught. Large-scale theft is in some ways a less rational crime to commit than murder. Why? Because if you kill somebody, the pain of the people affected (the relatives and friends) dies out in time. Five years after someone's friend is murdered the anguish is gone, but five years after somebody has stolen $700,000 there remains a reason for finding that person and getting that money back. Crimes of violence lead to a resolution of emotions. Crimes involving money don't lead to anything but perpetual desire to get the money back. It might appear that it would be easy to hide the theft of $700,000 by fleeing to Brazil, but all of the benefits of stealing it in the first place would have evaporated. The thief would be in perpetual hiding, since the people who lost the money would probably be willing to spend up to half the amount to recover it. A hundred thousand dollars is enough to find almost anybody anywhere in the world, or at least to make life so miserable that the thief would never enjoy the fruits of his stealing.

An interesting aspect of pursuing embezzlers is the attitude of insurance companies and other companies involved with fraud. Something not publicized, but known to most criminologists and people involved in prosecuting thieves, is that if it's clear and demonstrated but not provable that a particular person stole money, it is considered appropriate to "frame" him and put him in jail for a term as long as he would have served for the actual crime. For example, if you stole a large sum from the bank and the investigator knew for certain that you had stolen it but couldn't prove it, you can be certain you'd be kidnapped and would turn up in some Mediterranean country with dope on you, some place where dope is punishable by ten years in jail.

They feel it would be worth it to pay several thousand dollars to fly you there and leave you in that condition. There is a presumption within the fraud field that every thief must be punished. The principle for this is that the people who are tracking you down must be dissuaded from the temptation of stealing themselves, since they are often in the position to do so.

This started with a discussion of the trigger point that each person needs to find out about in order to keep him from the temptation that leads to financial crime. I covered a range of topics designed to scare you—to let you know that smart people don't embezzle and that the forces working against the embezzler are powerful. (I think I overdid it.)

Back to the ethics of money, its rules, and paying attention to it.

Part of "paying attention" to your money deals with debt. By debt I mean both large loans and small bills, the latter being situations where you have used something (gas, phone, space, etc.) and owe the institution that sold it to you.

Having debts and paying bills is not only useful but in many instances an effective way of making you "pay attention" to money, helping you to control yourself. Let me explain that in more detail.

When I was a banker I did a study on the potential market for an automatic bill-paying service for the bank's customers. I found out that people have a very strong resistance to automatic bill paying. Ostensibly, their reason was that they didn't want the bank to get involved in their personal life. Knowing how much anguish is involved in bill paying, however, I doubted that was the real reason. Probing further into how people pay their bills, I found that bill paying had several interesting hidden qualities. First of all, people used their bill paying as a way of punishing other people. A dentist or an interior decorator who hadn't done a very good job was certain not to receive payment for two, three or six months. This use of money as a form of punishment in the payment of bills was something people actually relished.

The second interesting thing was that people like to know the total amount of their bills, because this acts as a brake, a way of helping them control their future spending. If a man knew in February that his cash income was $500 and his still unpaid bills from Christmas totaled $800, he would restrain himself from buying that electric saw he wanted. The emotional weight of the bills would be a powerful restriction on his compulsion to buy, a way of controlling his whims and desires, a very powerful brake. The third aspect of paying bills was that people needed to know the sequence and urgency of their bills. They knew how long the phone company would allow them to go without cutting off their phone, that the garbage people would wait six months before stopping collection, and they knew that the utility company would let them go up to 90 days without paying. Each bill has a certain length of time that it can go without being paid. So if one of the children ended up having a $600 dental bill and the dentist wouldn't do the rest of the work until he had a payment of $200, then the bill payer would make the $200 payment and reschedule the payment of all of his other bills. He was thus able, in effect, to borrow from his other creditors. If a relative died and he had to fly to Portland, he could leave with the full knowledge that the utility, gas, phone and garbage bills would wait. In essence, he would be able to get a two hundred dollar loan simply by manipulating the sequence in which he paid his bills.

What I found about paying bills, then, is that it's part of how people, including me, control themselves and their "hard to control desires." I have mentioned each of the ways that I found people use to pay their bills in the hope that in reading about them we can all become conscious of how we pay bills ourselves and consequently can all do a better job of it.

As I mentioned a few pages back, bills and loans are related. I think a strong argument can be given in favor of certain kinds of loans. One reason that I accept in my own daily life is that a loan can be a form of forced savings. Life insurance people validly argue that a good reason for having life insurance is that it's hard for people to save. Most people have rosy views of their future, and scaring them into buying life insurance is a way to help them force themselves to save.

Two years ago I borrowed $2,000 from a bank where I could get a low interest rate (because I was a former banker), put it into a savings and loan, and started paying it off on a monthly basis over a two year period. The net effect was that at the end of two years I had $2,000 in savings.

It cost me only 2% per year to accomplish. (2% was the net difference of what I paid on the loan and the interest I received on the savings account.) I did this with the full knowledge that I was improving my credit standing for future emergencies. (Somewhere in the back of my mind I was telling myself that I had to be a good boy and make these payments, which I did.) That was forced savings. Essentially, a home mortgage or similar loan is much the same thing, a recognition that we need controls on our "desires."

Most of us seem to need limits. If you don't think you do then consider a test. See how easy it is for you to think of the next thing that you *want*. If you can spend three days and not think of the next thing that you want, you're right—you don't need self-imposed limits. However, if you want a new tape recorder, a Pakistani coin, or a new windmill for your water pump, restrictions are going to be necessary within your life and within your life-style.

As I have been writing this there has been a schism in my mind. On the one hand, I realize that nearly every reader has the problem of lack of money control—even an enormous percentage of people who really *think* they don't. On the other hand, there are a *few* people who really don't have needs and desires other than rudimentary ones. Those few include people willing to live anywhere, eat beans or rice or go three days without eating. Usually they devote their lives to something other than their personal whims. They range from a priest in a Zen center to a devoted nurse aiding the indigent dying. My advice has to be useful for both groups, the overwhelming majority and the exceptional few.

A very simple way to keep track of money is to have a checking account—

something absolutely, unassailably essential for the vast majority of people. Even with the slightest effort you can find a bank that either doesn't charge you or requires a small minimum balance. I have heard the argument that "if I only use cash, I can't spend more than I earn." The logic is fine in the few instances where a person is earning $200.00 a week and spends it on having a good time. However, in most instances where you have responsibilities it pays to have a checking account. It's a very simple way of keeping track of what you spend money on, which is an important part of the Second Law. It also creates a consciousness of your money-related behavior, putting it all in a sort of perspective.

There are two approaches that are useful in balancing your checkbook. One is to get two checking accounts—especially if they are cheap or free. Then one month you write checks out of one check book and the next month you write out of the other. What will happen is that leaving one account fallow will allow all the checks to clear, leaving your bank balance the same as your checkbook. Another approach is to *add* in your checkbook instead of subtracting. I discovered this from some ingenious suburban housewives. Say you deposit $160.00. Instead of subtracting the amount of each check, you simply enter the amount of the checks as you write them and total them until they reach $160.00. It's much easier to add than it is to subtract — and faster.

I'd like to talk about people, and the way we handle money. How the ethic of money permeates our lives.

I have a friend whom I call "130% Jack." One of Jack's characteristics is that he always claims he can get you a deal, but whatever Jack's deal is you can be sure that it will cost 30% more than the normal retail price. Jack, however, actually believes that he's saving you money. Jack is well paid, spends an enormous amount of money on drugs, and is sort of muddle headed. He has a general belief that money will take care of itself, a kind of misreading of the First Law. It's a misreading because he violates the Second Law, which deals with our personal lives and which implies a sort of neatness, an ability to organize, a coherence. Ultimately, the money ethic deals with our responsibility for our own lives, although our dealing with the money ethic usually remains on the periphery of living, indicating a sort of sleepiness. I'm not objecting to this, or moralizing about it, but rather suggesting that paying attention to the details of our lives is part of understanding who we are, and part of growing. Our inattentiveness toward money is enough of a misperception of reality that it can lead us into trouble, in the same sense that any misperception of reality can lead to trouble.

Jack leads a sheltered life, with a soft job among friends. His operating reality is presently close enough to the reality in his own mind so that things are O.K. But, in general, most of the world requires a perception of reality which involves a much more careful attention to money. Jack's friends are tolerant, but in a lower income level he might be considered an unfair dealer and end up being stabbed. On another level, in the business world, he would be considered an untrustworthy person, with his 130% deals. Fortunately for Jack, he is living in a situation where reality and his perception of reality are close enough.

However, the fact that Jack smoked hash before scuba diving and almost drowned convinced me that the perceived reality reflected in his handling of money is only part of a pervasive view of the world around him. It shows that he has a general misperception of operating reality. The handling of money deals with an ethic, and ethics permeate the entire thing that we call "personality."

Can you change someone like Jack, who has such a characteristic? The analogy of Alcoholics Anonymous in Gregory Bateson's book *Steps to an Ecology of Mind* could be applied here. Bateson says that Alcoholics Anonymous works when a person finally accepts that for the rest of his life he is going to be an alcoholic. He has to operate from that position and never go near a drink. He has to realize that not even after five years of being off booze will he be less of an alcoholic, that there is no such thing as an intelligent alcoholic who can control himself. Only when he realizes that there's nothing he can do, can he survive.

Perhaps Bateson's theory isn't true for everyone. Frank was exactly what you'd expect an embezzler to be. He was a 26-year-old bachelor in San Diego who lived so high that I was always astounded. Frank was very open about describing how he had ingeniously arranged to shift his finances around. For example, he was on the loan committee of a savings and loan company. Because of his position on the loan committee, a bank that was affiliated with the savings and loan lent him enough money to buy a fancy Jaguar XKE. He was able to borrow on a 30-month payment plan with a balloon at the end (meaning that the bulk of the principal didn't have to be paid back until the end of the loan period). This is, of course, an extremely bad lending policy, because by the end of the 30-month period the value of the car would be negligible and the source of income to pay it off might not be around. It turned out that Frank was embezzling from his S & L by making loans to himself in the names of several customers. He was discovered when he left the country for a short vacation. He had a friend mail his monthly payments, but unfortunately for Frank his friend was six days late in sending in the money. Automatic notices went out from the computer to the people in whose names the loans were made. They came into the S & L very irate because they knew nothing about the loan. Frank was promptly caught.

Frank had what is known as chutzpah. After he was caught he tried to get himself sent to a nice minimum-security prison in Arizona, but, alas, the judge wasn't so nice, and he was sent to Terminal Island Prison in Los Angeles for one year. After Frank got out he couldn't get any job whatsoever, since he had been trained only as a banker and now had an embezzlement conviction and jail term behind him. He was at his wits' end for more than a year. He might well have ended up a circus barker if it weren't for the fact that he came to an unusual self-understanding. He ran an ad in the *Wall Street Journal* which read FORMER EMBEZZLER AVAILABLE FOR WORK. In the ad he briefly explained his background and what he went to jail for. He got over thirty responses to his ad. I would tend to agree with most of the people who attempted to hire him—somebody who fully recognizes what he had done is capable of controlling his future behavior.

Frank turned out to be quite successful. Within a year he was living very well on the Spanish Riviera—as the result of a good salary, his reward for being a competent financier.

In addition to the rule that you must keep track of your money, it's important to know who you are and where you are in money terms. This comes out most clearly when you apply for a loan—although it applies less to individuals than to projects and businesses.

One of the first things I do when I'm

acting as a financial consultant for a client is to get him to the point where he is eligible for a bank loan. I recommend this also for non-profit bodies, sometimes encouraging *part* of a non-profit organization to apply for a loan, often collateralized by the rest of the organization. Now, why do I do this? Because the whole process of getting a loan is a powerful way of getting insight into what your business or project is. Bankers are generally clear-sighted, narrow, and unimaginative, which is fine, since the bank's purpose is to make 100% secured loans without taking any risks whatsoever. Risk-taking in banking is incompetence. If you feel that banks should take risks with their money then you probably have a misconception of what the function of a bank is. Banks do lend to many other institutions like finance companies, retail stores and others which *are* in the business of taking risks with their loanable funds. But the bank is the wholesaler and tries to have zero risk. In fact, any time a bank gets much above 3/10ths of 1% loss in its general lending it is being poorly operated, and this is pretty close to being no loss at all.

What are we doing, then, when we take someone to a bank? We are saying that he or she has enough perception of the money reality in which he operates to be able to say something about his future, with virtually no risk implied. In order to say something about his future, people have to have a pretty accurate perception of themselves.

In the case of my private clients, once they have this self-perception I make it clear that the first thing to do is get to know the loan officer at the bank, and this involves time. Usually it takes as much as a year for a banker to get to know you.

What do you do when you go to the bank for a loan? You prepare three things:

a general financial statement, a projection, and a personal financial statement.

1. A general financial statement applies to a business or a project. You might want one for your personal money keeping practices. It's an accurate record of what you have done up to date. It includes a balance sheet and an income and expense statement.

It would be easy to show you a picture of a balance sheet or an income-expense statement, but if I put one in the book most people flipping through the pages would be scared shitless and never read it. So I'll try to describe one with words. (If you actually have to do one, get a book with a picture of one in it.)

The balance sheet generally has three sections: assets, liabilities and net worth.

a) Assets are cash in the bank on the day of the statement, money people owe you, and the value of physical things such as a building or an inventory. They are usually listed in descending order from the most liquid to the least liquid—liquid meaning how fast an item can be turned into cash. For example, collecting a debt of $200 might take a month, but selling your chicken coop for cash might take five years.

b) Liabilities are what you owe. They, too, are listed in descending order— from the most pressing item needing to be paid to the least pressing. Under liabilities comes your phone bill and rent, the accumulated payroll to the date of the statement, what you owe the bank, and last of all the loan you promised to repay your cousin if the project succeeds.

c) Net worth is what you get if you subtract what you owe (liabilities) from your assets. It can be negative in some cases.

An income-expense statement is just that. At the top is listed your income over the last period of time (a month, quarter, or year); below that are your expenses for the same period. At the bottom is the difference between expense and income, either a surplus or a deficit. Income is the total money that came in. Expenses are everything that you wrote checks for, including payroll, business trips to Mazatlan, and the clay urn at the front door that you bought on your trip. A balance sheet is a snapshot of you, your project or your business at *one* point in time; it's just as if you should empty your pockets and count what's in them, figure out the value of your sweater, shoes and Swiss army knife and write it all down on a piece of paper. An income-expense statement is a history of what happened.

What is a balance sheet for? Anything—profit making, a non-profit venture, even a picture of your personality and behavior can be put on a balance sheet. It's a way of letting a banker know, in clear terms, what you've done. By studying the structure of your financial statements he can ask intelligent questions and get even more information. That is exactly what a banker is trained to do—to look at ratios, the relationship between money in one part of your statement and money in some other part. This simply leads him to ask logical questions, and from seeing a certain ratio he'll ask the same question of a Company that is hundreds of millions of dollars in debt that he'll ask of you.

2. The second thing you need is a projection. A projection is usually an estimate of future income and expenses. In most cases it is simply a straight-line forecast of the future based on past experience. Although it is simple it is very significant. To be able to project what is

going to happen means that you have an understanding of your existing reality. That is why it is valuable to get people to go to a bank for a loan—because they are required to make a projection, which in turn requires the examination of themselves in enough detail to be able to understand their operating reality.

Let me give you an example of what I do with the clients I work with and their projects. We sit down together and make a projection. We work together because as an outsider I can look at their future more objectively than they can, not being as optimistic as they are in hoping for good revenues or in thinking that they can keep expenses from going up. The result is that I am able to help them look more closely at their present situation, to give them a better sense of their capabilities and of what they are doing. This helps them to face what their activities are realistically and to confront their operating reality. Being forced to make projections requires them to get an overall view of the interacting forces within their organization. The projection is particularly powerful because it requires an understanding of some of the major forces involved in the business.

The really surprising thing about a projection is that it is extremely simple. Once you have made one or two you will be amazed at how simple it is to do and yet how powerful it can be in affecting your understanding.

Let's start with the simplest way to do one. Take your past growth rate, sales and expenses, and assume that this rate will be the same for the coming period—let's say a year. Suppose you grew from last year to this year by 20% in revenues and 18% in expenses. Simply project these percentages for the coming year and break them down so that for each month you get equal increases in revenue and expenses. Now, this is unrealistic because you know that revenues and expenses vary on a month-by-month basis, so go back and look at your seasonal patterns. Did you do better in August? Is November a bad month? This process can be a powerful eye-opener. A number of my clients became conscious for the first time that there was a pattern that business was bad in September and October, for example, and extremely good in November and December. They may have known this intuitively but they had not actually seen the consequences of these fluctuations on paper. A strong awareness of their situation made it possible for them to borrow from the bank well in advance of their need and to pay back their loan promptly. This helped to establish extremely good relations with the bank because it indicated that they understood their business and had enough vision to enable them to anticipate problems. Understanding the cyclic patterns of revenues and expenses can make a big difference.

Sometimes when you look at expenses you feel a little uneasy about some that seem high or others that look too low. This is a signal to go back to see what the relationships are. You might find that when revenues go up in March, labor costs go up in May. You are now forced to look at some of the interrelationships in your business. In many companies these may not be so obvious (they may well be intuitive), but as you look at them you will find patterns that are important in understanding what to do.

In making projections I have often been extraordinarily accurate in predicting both revenues and expenses—sometimes within 1% or 2% per month. Clients have been baffled by this, and I smile enigmatically. The fact is that any fairly good projection in a situation where conditions are pretty stable will be surprisingly accurate. I think you've got the point.

3. The third thing you prepare for the bank is a personal financial statement. This is a very useful thing for most people, because in many situations there is an intricate relationship between the principal individual and the project or business. In reality they are integrated, although legally they are separated. Looking at a personal balance sheet gives a person a significantly better understanding of who he is and how much he is devoting to his project or his business, and essentially what his life-time commitment is. Is he paying himself a lot and putting very little back? Is he increasing his personal worth in terms of cars and houses, or is he depleting his savings and building up the market value of his company? A personal financial statement is a useful tool because it confronts you visually with what the banker will be looking

for. He wants to see what the relationship is between you and your commitment, your energy and your passion.

It's worthwhile making a personal financial statement periodically. I suggest you make a copy of each statement so you can go back and make comparisons with each new one.

Taking all these things to the bank is probably one of the most powerful exercises in personal growth; its power is magnified when one realizes that a relationship with the bank is something that extends over a period of time. The concrete value of a "projection sheet" is being able to show someone else (the bank) that you have goals and visions and that you are able to relate to them over a period of time. It is a way of saying that your perceived reality and your operating reality are pretty close to each other in terms of money. It's also a demonstration to the banker that you are capable of judging yourself, and judging yourself fairly accurately.

I'll use some specific examples of my clients and what happened in their relationships with the banks. In the first case Sal, at the time I became his advisor was in extremely bad shape financially, heavily in debt to the bank (very poor sales revenue) and with all bills more than 90 days past due. By helping him prepare the kinds of materials that the banker now required I was able to help him understand his business realistically and to give him a sense of what was economically feasible. I also helped him to understand what had to be done, how much sales he had to generate, and to what extent he had to work late and on weekends to keep his actual out-of-pocket labor costs from driving him out of business.

We went to the bank, and the banker was very impressed with our careful analysis. The bank had at least two choices.

It could demand full payment of the loan at that time and put Sal out of business (both he and the bank would have lost in that case), or it could try to find some solution that would allow Sal to stay in business. Now remember that the bank could have closed Sal's business down in hopes of getting some of the assets which were there. Banks are usually the first ones in line when it comes to dividing up the property of a creditor. But in this case the bank agreed to reduce the amount of each payment required to repay Sal's loan.

Sal also did something that he had never done before. He started paying by check, delivering it to the banker in person on the day it was due—or sometimes even a day before. He did this for six months, giving absolute, utter priority to this responsibility, paying the bank before he paid all other bills—including his own salary. At the end of the six months we had not only achieved the goals set out in the financial projection but the banker was so personally satisfied with the delivery of payments that he willingly extended the payment schedule for the balance, allowing Sal to accumulate enough money to bring all other back debts current. This was no friendly country banker who reacted so well, incidentally; it was the Bank of America. Within seven months after I had become Sal's financial advisor he was relatively debt free.

My second client's experience was similar, but in his case he needed to get a bank loan, not to pay one off. At the time I took him on as a client Sheldon was well beyond the point of bankruptcy, although none of his creditors knew it. He had a great deal of money coming in, but he was past due in paying nearly all his bills. He was living on borrowed time, capitalizing his company on his creditors' money. Sheldon didn't have any personal resources left, having already poured them into the company to get it started. His company had a relatively large swing in sales revenue. On top of this, as more business came in more capital was needed to cover labor costs until the revenue from the sale of products was received—a fairly typical growth business problem.

Since investors, his only possible source of money, were unlikely to help because the firm was in an unglamorous and highly specialized field, he could only turn to a bank.

The first year that I worked with Sheldon's company we sent all his financial statements to local banks, indicating a desire for a bank loan. He was treated as coldly as anyone could conceivably be. In most cases the banks said, "Very nice to meet you. Hope to see you again. Let us know if we can ever be of any help." One year later, however, through simple, careful attention to the books and careful control of expenses (with regular planning sessions about sales), the company made a miraculous turnaround. We went back to the banks, this time with new financial statements, and, although the reader probably won't believe this, the bankers literally hugged my client. They were so impressed with the change in financial conditions that they asked for the opportunity to make a loan. One of the banks ended up by offering to make an unsecured loan for a substantial amount any time Sheldon needed one. Today Sheldon knows how to use this line of credit, and he uses it frequently. He has been able to expand his business without outside capital and to maintain complete control of his own company. He can grow on borrowed bank money, as he well deserves, because of the amount of time and energy he has put into the firm so far. The lesson of this is that his financial figures and his relationship with the bank were very important. The bank lending relationship requires an understanding of yourself and an accurate enough picture of reality to allow you to operate effectively.

I'd like to explain three terms that I just used: capitalization, investor, and unsecured loan. Capitalization is the core money that a business or an individual has to fall back upon for either emergencies or for business expansion. For example, you are producing about $400 worth of special sandals in a rural community in Arizona. You buy your leather for $200. The money you receive in sales is more than enough to allow you to buy next month's leather. The orders you get are not so great that you couldn't double your shoe production if you wanted to, because you've got enough leather on hand and can wait the extra month it takes for all the letters with payment to come back. Everything is running smoothly when all of a sudden an article about your sandals appears in *The New Yorker*. Your orders, instead of being $400 worth a month, jump to $15,000 a month. The leather you need now would cost you $6,000 but you have only $400 in the bank. So you're stuck. There aren't going to be any bankers around your part of the country who will know how reliable those thousands of readers are who have placed orders for your shoes. They will probably be unwilling to advance you the money because they don't know you; you've never been in their bank and you don't have an account there. There's almost no chance that you are going to be able to do anything but send out letters to all the people who ordered sandals saying, "I'm sorry we can't produce your shoes unless you want to send us some money in advance." Since very few people will actually be willing to do that, you're in trouble. The money that you need is for capitalization—money for expansion. In this case it's the money you use to finance other people's credit.

Another example would be where your shoe business is humming along beautifully, producing $15,000 worth of sandals a month, when one of your major buyers, a department store in Los Angeles that buys $5,000 worth a month, starts having financial trouble and is now paying 50 to 60 days late. You know the rest of your sales will continue, but if your labor costs and your leather costs can't be cut down, or your sales to the department store stopped, you might go out of business. Once again, the bank doesn't know you and doesn't know the Los Angeles department store. It is theoretically possible that on some written guarantee from the department store, if its credit was extremely good—and if the bank knew you—the bank would lend you the money. (This is the reason to get to know your banker; banks make loans mostly to people they know.) The money you need for the one or two months in order to continue payments for leather and labor while awaiting payment from the department store would have to come from somewhere. This is why you need capital, to serve as a reserve for just such an emergency.

Then there's the concept of *investor*. In general, an investor is somebody who puts up money in return for future income. Anyone can be an investor, whether he has no net worth or a lot of wealth. There is no special amount of money that makes one an investor. In Japan an investor is often a member of a large syndicate of people from different walks of life who all put equal amounts of money into a large investment pool. In South Africa an investor can be a laborer who joins other laborers who migrate to work for six months, all of them pooling their wages in order to purchase a small business upon their return.

The concept of an investor is different from that of a lender. A lender gives you his money, and after a certain period of time he gets all of it back with interest in addition. There is an explicit, if not written agreement that the money loaned is not being risked and that there will be interest paid for its use. An investor, on the other hand, takes the same risks as the individual who is directly responsible for the enterprise he invests in. He will gain back in proportion to the amount of risk that he has assumed.

An acquaintance of mine makes an illegal little device that you put on your telephone so a person calling you won't get billed for his call. He can build the units for $10 apiece and sells them for $40. When he produces forty, for a total gross revenue of $1600, he just about covers all of his expenses, including labor.

When he got started he needed $400 to buy the electronic components. There were two ways he could have gotten it — he could either have found an investor or have borrowed the money. If he had had to borrow it he would have had to take a bank loan at 8% interest for a year, which means that on the $400 he would only have had to pay back $420 after a year. Well, he doesn't deal with bankers, so he had to borrow four hundred dollars for two months and pay back $450. Such a loan had to be from someone who knew and trusted him, the $50 fee compensating for his friend's inconvenience.

An investor, on the other hand, is someone who would have said "Look, I'll give you the $400, but I want to share in your profit. You'll be getting $1,200 out of this product. A lot of it goes to reward you for your time, but a lot of it repays you for the risk you take in doing an illegal thing. For my four hundred dollars I'll

take the risk along with you, one of the
risks being that the phone company
might develop a way to detect your de-
vices and after that no one would want to
buy any more. One other risk is that you
might get arrested. Because of this I want
10% of your net return after cost." That
would be 10% of $1,200, which would be
a return of $120 on his $400 if everything
went well.

In the case of the person who receives
a *loan* there is an implied responsibility.
If this acquaintance who makes the telephone gadgets is honest, he'd spend a lot
of time over the next six or eight months
repaying his lender even if the deal fell
through. Even if he went to jail he'd be
obligated to repay the loan as soon as he
got out.

Finally, loans fall into the category of
either "secured" or "unsecured." In case
of a secured loan the lender has a specific
object in mind that the borrower will

have to sell to make up for the loan in case he can't repay it. A pawn shop deals in secured loans—but here there is a highly unusual relationship between the price of the merchandise and the amount of the loan. For example, you could take a $600 typewriter to a pawn broker but you might be able to borrow only $50 on it—a pretty bad ratio. At a bank, however, a $13,000 car generally entitles you to borrow $10,000 assuming that you have insurance to make sure the car is repaired if it is ever damaged.

A credit card account is an example of an unsecured loan. If you can't repay the debt you create, the credit card company has no specific thing of yours to sell, so they will try to raise the money by attaching your wages or in other ways, which can involve the courts, bankruptcy, etc. Because there's generally more risk involved in a loan that is unsecured the lender usually charges more interest. If one of the businesses described a few pages back should go into bankruptcy, an outstanding (still unpaid) secured loan would give the bank greater rights over the property to be liquidated than an unsecured loan would.

While we are at it, here are two other concepts which many people balk at or grow up failing to comprehend: "gross" and "net." Gross has a pretty standard meaning. It's the final price in a production chain of a product or service. An example: the price of this book as sold over the counter is its gross price. If you want to know gross receipts for the sale of the book, it would be the number of books sold times that price. Suppose we sold 100,000 paperback books at $6.00 each, then $600,000 would be the gross revenue on this book.

The same is true of any item. Gross is the largest number relating to the amount of the sale. From the gross amount other expenses or other percentages are subtracted, leaving the "net." Anything less than the gross is a net. So if somebody talks about a net you have to find out what net he means. Net has no specific meaning. For example, the net percentage the publisher might expect to get on this book is 10%, which is 10% of the retail gross price, $6.00. Someone else might be talking about the net of something else—say the net of what the bookseller pays the publisher for the book. He may pay only $2.40 for the book, so if somebody was talking about 10% of *that* net figure it would be substantially different than 10% of the gross. If you hear the term net, find out what it refers to. If you hear the term gross, you don't have to be told what it is.

Accounting is a field in which technical words usually have a sound reason for their existence: they are shorthand for concepts that are regularly used. Actually, very few words in the accounting or economics field are designed to be mystifying or obscure; you simply have to learn the concepts so that you can use them.

Before I close this chapter there are a few bits of Ann Landers-type advice that I would like to add.

When you open a checking account, open it with the largest amount of money you possibly can. I'm not kidding! Even if the average balance in your account is only going to be $50, try to borrow a friend's $10,000 (home down payment) for *one day* so you can use it to open your account. You don't have to go that far, but anything over a couple of thousand dollars looks good. You can withdraw most of the money a few days after the account is opened. Really! The reason for this is that the bank records your opening balance on your signature card (and often in other places, too), believing that it is representative of your financial status. I did a study when I was a banker and found absolutely no correlation between opening balances and the kind of balances that appeared later on in the same account. It's such a strong tradition to do it this way (at least a hundred years old) that bankers still judge people by their opening balance. Try it; the branch manager will smile on you forever more.

It may seem middle-class to have credit, but if you have it you need less money. "Credit" is the ability to borrow, and if your credit is good you don't need savings—or at least you need less savings. Savings are generally for emergencies, but if you have credit you can use it in an emergency instead of your savings, and pay it back later.

All it takes to establish credit is a little time and a little stability. You need *one* job, one address, a phone and a checking account for one year. Having decided to establish a good credit rating and already having a job and an address, wait four months and then apply for a gasoline credit card. Next apply for credit at a luxury store (they give credit *very* readily because their losses on credit are covered by the high mark-up on their merchandise). After six months apply at Sears or Macy's or a similar middle-price-range national store. Their credit is the very hardest to get and can really get you the rest. Use these credit accounts once or twice and pay promptly. After from seven to nine months you can apply for MasterCard or Visa (not both at the same time). When you get them your credit is really established (after a few months, you can ask by letter to have your credit card borrowing amount raised). Now you are free — you can get a new job as often as you wish and move as often as you feel like it; your credit is established. Just remember to pay your accounts promptly, and never have a run-in with a jewelry store! Most bad credit ratings are put in the credit rating computers by jewelry stores—the $300-diamond-studded-watch-type places.

Credit is dependent mostly on stability. Your stability is measured by the time you stay with a job (they check), the time you have lived at your present and previous residence, whether or not you have a phone (bad debtors usually avoid having their own phone), and by your checking account. Be sure not to overdraw your checking account more than once or twice a year: sometimes your bank may keep track of it, and sometimes the word gets around to other banks.

Lastly, if you need a loan, shop around. The bigger the loan, the more important this is. Banks are not monolithic; each branch is different. Some have loan officers or managers who are liberal, smart and understanding; others have insensitive bores who retired at age twenty-four when they joined the bank.

Ask around. If you need a loan for a specialized purpose find someone who got a similar loan and go to their lender. Specialized knowledge and good experience on past loans are what encourage a lender to make additional loans in esoteric areas.

MONEY IS A DREAM.

A Fantasy as Alluring as the Pied Piper

MONEY IS VERY much a state of mind. It's much like the states of consciousness that you see on an acid trip. Maybe it is the animal figure seen in the peyote dream (Mescalito). It is fantasy in itself, purely a dream. People who go after it as though it were real and tangible, say a person who is trying to earn a hundred thousand dollars, orients their life and ends up in such a way as to have been significantly changed simply to reach that goal. They become part of that object and since the object is a dream (a mirage) they become quite different from what they set out to be.

To really understand the extent to which money is a dream listen to the economist's definition of money, it is *part of a system of relative pricing and an accounting store of value.* Let's take the second, a store of value. It is a record of previous transactions like your savings account, your checking account. These records are an indication of credits of labor, credits of energy or inheritance that you have built up. It is a store of imaginary value. When you think in terms of it as part of a relative pricing system the fantasy element becomes even more dramatic. In theoretical terms, the price of anything in this world is determined by the demand of everybody else in the world for that item in proportion to its scarcity. Money is the communication medium that records these pressures throughout the world. The abstract reason a pair of nylons costs $2.25 is because that is the relative demand for a particular pair of nylons, in *a* store (Macy's on May 15) in comparison to the needs of all the people in the world and available resources of those people relative to the other available resource demands for the production of those stockings. You can see from even the vaguest description of what money is that it must be a dream.

I hope you can realize that people who set goals that are related to money, are bound to follow a peculiar road the same way that someone in real life sets out to find the animal he or she saw on their last mescaline trip must inevitably stumble and bump into things and realize in the end that they have become something of a fantasy themselves in the search.

COMMENTARY ON THE THIRD LAW

The money that man uses everywhere in the world is the same. The yen, the pound, the dollar, the peso are all manipulated and function in the same way. The governments of the world try to regulate their supplies of money, and they all use similar theories. Money is one thing that we all have in common; it's a dream, an illusion, it's not real. *It is a relationship between all things in the world.* Just hearing myself say that reminds me of its dreamlike qualities.

I want to examine this dreamlike quality of money before I try to describe what happens to people who deal with it. Dreams have a number of qualities that relate to money. A dream is not something that can be placed in the past or the future. It is always immediate and present. A dream does things, as Gregory Bateson points out in *Steps to an Ecology of Mind*; it cannot be a negative. In a dream you don't say I am *not* going to the store. The dream acts out the negative and carries it to its conclusion, either absurd or fatal. For example, you go to the store, and a giant artichoke eats you.

Money doesn't have a past or a future, except in a very abstract way. Take, for example, your net worth, which is something you have accumulated over time. It may include something your parents accumulated, yet there's no particular piece of currency which embodies that time span. All you have is an abstract symbol of some events that occurred in the past; The money itself doesn't have attributes of the past. Money is always the present; it embodies no concept of future.

Economists over the past twenty years have come to realize that we cannot borrow from the future. Governments used to be accused of borrowing from future generations when they incurred enormous war debts; it was argued that future children would have to pay off those debts. It's now clear to economists that there is no way to borrow from the future.

The only wealth that exists is that which is currently available from the combination of labor, energy, tools and resources. You just cannot make future people or future resources available at the present, so money has the dream quality of having no future.

Let's have a look at money's lack of "negativeness." Money is nearly always related to action. We exchange things, we come to some sort of agreed price on the relative values of the things we exchange—and that's money (at least that's the price component of money). A debt, or negative net worth, is not really negative; it's just a direction of flow—from debtor to creditor. There's essentially no way to do something with money that is the equivalent of saying "Don't go to the store." (This is hard to grasp; it's a Zen koan like "not does not exist.") Money is just there. Similarly, you can't say something has no value, which would mean that it has no exchange price. Everything has an exchange value; somebody somewhere would want it at some sufficiently low price. My typing table doesn't have an innate value, but it does have a value in exchange. I can't make that value disappear by just saying it's going to disappear. On the other hand, I can only make it exist at the time I am going to exchange it.

Economists would point out that some things are treated as free—with no price—but they aren't. Air and ocean have been conventionally viewed that way. Of course, we are now paying for our idea that the air is free in the form of medical costs for lung cancer, auto pollution controls, and in countless other ways. We are paying higher prices for fish and working to clean our beaches because of our treatment of the ocean as a free thing.

To add to the picture of money as a

dream, look at its universality. It's the same in Zanzibar, Montreal, Bogalusa and Peru. Everywhere that man is he has price, capital, wholesale, retail, interest, profit, tax, cash vs. accrual, inflation and deflation. Something as complex as that is everywhere we are; only language seems to be as universal a human trait. Look at each word and how dreamlike it is—for example, inflation. Our government, 2,000 miles away from me, writes checks for more dollars than it receives in taxes and the money I have in my pocket decreases in value; it now costs me more to buy nearly everything.

I hope that all these rambling words can somehow convey to you that money is a dream. What might all this mean? If you chase after a dream, you will have a grasping clenched fist in the end and a sore hand with nothing in it. In a sense that's what happens to the kind of person who spends all his life seeking money.

He's seeking something that is unreal, that doesn't exist, and what he will end up with is a hollow existence. In the end he is not the same person he started out to be. Maybe someone can convince me otherwise by introducing me to a person whose goal was to make a lot of money and who ended up a whole and interesting person, but my experience with people who set out to make a lot of money is that when they get it they find there's very little they can do with it, or they have changed so much they are not at all what they wanted to be.

One of my close friends is an example of the fist clenching—money type whose fist is now empty. I've known Melissa for eleven years. I met her when she first opened her own art gallery. It was an excellent gallery and she was a first-rate painter. She was a bright, happy, warm person who was loved by many and who had become the center of an exciting circle of friends. As she learned the gallery business she found that she was good at sales and very good at her business. It grew, and her little spark of interest in getting enough money to run a nice gallery became a flaming passion for big business. She is earning lots of money now—her business has expanded beyond the art gallery but she is a different person. I no longer feel comfortable around her. She talks about her fancy sports car, her home in the country, her foreign buying trips, and mostly about how well her business is doing. She's not very happy. She has few friends, narrow interests; she goes through men like a hurricane through a corn field. She rarely paints anymore, and she works long hours at money making. I stayed with her for a while recently and saw what a lonely person she has become and what a tyrant she is with her employees.

Another person worth describing is

Judy. Judy was a hard working, warm woman from an upper-middle-class background. Somewhere along the line she decided she wanted to become rich, and for her that meant a rich lover. She found one, and, now she lives in villas around the world, buys new dresses for every big party and is au courant on all the latest fads of the jet set. We find her difficult to be with. She can talk about little else but butlers, maids and the problems of wealth, and she doesn't like the man she lives with.

These sound like stereotypes but they're not. Nor are the people in such situations necessarily unhappy. What happens, though, is that their worship of money changes them to such an extent that the quest for money becomes their whole life.

There is a positive aspect of dreams and fantasy. I think it is the realization that a fantasy can stretch your priorities.

Fantasy is a way of challenging your own conventional and immediate value structure. For instance, people often talk to me about having a piece of land where they can go to get away from it all and live peacefully. I can show these people how they can get their land in less than a year. They will have to sacrifice a number of things in order to be able to get it, but suggesting that they strive for their fantasy will lead to an examination of their priorities. The same applies to almost anything. An 18 year old woman was telling me last week that she wanted a new ElDorado. I could have told her how she could get an ElDorado by not buying any new dresses for a year, by working an extra three hours a week and maybe by doing some "Avon calling" on Wednesday evenings. That kind of fantasy, realistically examined, would force her to ask herself about her other priorities—such as how important a new dress is to her, or how important is living in a $800 apartment compared to living with three other people and spending only $200 a month.

In most cases, no change in the availability of money is going to change a person's priorities. People usually know what they want to do, but they're unwilling to acknowledge whatever it is within their personality that makes them do what they're doing and leads to their self deception. It is certainly not money that puts them where they are. People invariably have scapegoats, and money has always been one of the most convenient ones—because it is commonly agreed that we can't do most of the things we want to do because we don't have enough money. As long as the majority of us believe that, it may be a useful, convenient mirage. Unfortunately in some other cultures it's been the Jews who supposedly kept things from happening, and thus people (the Germans and Poles, for example) set out to kill the Jews. I think the money scapegoat might be a little better one for a culture to believe in, because it's pretty hard to kill money.

Later on, under Laws Five and Six, I'll tell about my experiences in giving. At this point, however, to emphasize that money is a dream-thing, I'd like to relate one of the most powerful experiences I gained from being on the board of POINT, whose origins are in the surplus money from the *Whole Earth Catalog* created by Stewart Brand. POINT is a non-profit foundation that gives grants. The board deliberately made unrestricted money available to all board members in order to find out what it would do to us. I have come to realize that nothing I ever wanted to do has been prevented because of lack of money. What I did with the POINT money however, was to accelerate actually doing some of the things I had wanted to do, which let me get out of my system a couple of the things that proved to be trivial. (Until they were done, however, I didn't realize that they were trivial.)

For example, the money allowed me to build some sex furniture—therapeutic furniture—so that people could have sex in more positions than are possible by just lying on a flat bed. I had been thinking about his furniture for nine years. Finally, when I built the furniture I found that nobody wanted to use it. The availability of the money allowed my fantasy to become a reality, and something that had essentially been operating as a bottleneck in my mind was dispensed with. I had always had enough money for this project; it was just that I never used it. The idea was like a mental loop that kept going around and around, slowing me down on other things and affecting my development, a minor thing on my mind's back burner that had kept me from doing other major things. The access to money, to be able to do anything I wanted, didn't change my plans or my reality significantly. It did make me realize that money does not play a role in setting personal goals or in evaluating the world around you. Having access to money for any purpose helps to get some of the cobwebs out of the way. To get rid of all those cobwebs probably didn't cost more than $2,000, money which in the past I had occasionally had in savings.

Interestingly, one of the things that I had considered to be relatively minor—carving a mile-long sign in the desert with a tractor for observation by satellites—taught me a whole new lesson. In the struggle to get the project done I learned about how important a sense of "adventure" is. In carrying out the project I used heavy equipment and flying, and there were some risks and dangers involved. Almost all of my skills—as a pilot, a mathematician, a planner, a scientist, a friend, and a mystic—were required for this project. The whole thing gave me a taste of adventure, and it was spectacular, for I learned the importance of adventure in everyday life and how devastating the absence of it can be in creating boredom. Another thing I learned from the project was that some of my concepts weren't really as outrageous as I'd thought. I came to view it later as conceptual art and not just as a social consciousness project. From my desert sign adventure, close ties with a number of important conceptual artists developed, and new ideas in conceptual art evolved.

Now this was a small project, but in many ways the stumbling block aspect of it was such that I had to get it out of the way, and in the process of getting it out of the way I learned a great deal more about myself.

Having access to POINT Foundation money was like waking up from a dream. It takes very little to wake up from a dream, to realize the difference between a dream state and reality. If only everybody could live out the fantasy of having a million dollars, we might see a radically different world. If we could just begin to operate on that basis it could have significant effects on our lives.

The Next Time You Visit a Bank. Just walk into any bank, whether you're known there or not, go to the center of the lobby, keeping your hands at your side, stop, take about two minutes to turn around slowly and look at everything. Now, how do you feel? I'd be surprised if you would have feelings that strong even in a church. A bank is a modern day sacred place, and it evokes very strong culturally-ingrained reactions. Three things from my experience illustrate this. First, as a banker I occasionally had reason to visit branch offices, sometimes taking friends with me. I would go behind the teller line for some reason, simply lifting the latch (I've never seen one that was secured by anything more than a simple latch) and walk through. My guests, however, wouldn't go near the back of the teller line; it was a taboo area. I could never even get them to put their little toe across.

Second, no promotion, scheme or display attracts attention when placed in a lobby. Paintings on display never sell, unless they are hanging near the loan officers' desks where people sitting down have a chance to look at them. Even a TV set turned on during the World Series doesn't attract attention, unless it's in a window so people can see it from outside or in a corner far away from the bank transaction area.

Third and finally, a sociologist, Jane Prather, worked with me on a project where she was employed as a teller for three months. Jane noticed that within twelve feet of the bank entrance 95% of the customers would act in some way to show that they had a reason for being in the bank—like taking a pen out of a purse or reaching into a pocket for a wallet. And, of course, while waiting in line people almost never looked anywhere except straight ahead. Maybe we're all crooks and feel guilty about being in a bank.

Yeh, a bank is a strange place.

MONEY IS
A NIGHTMARE.

In Jail, Robbery, Fears of Poverty

ABOUT NINETY PERCENT of all crimes
are committed because of money (I
looked this up a few days ago), and about
eighty percent of all people in jail are
there because of money-related crimes.
Eighty percent of all crimes consist of
robbery, burglary, larceny, forgery and
auto theft. A few other things which push
the percentage even higher are murders,
especially family murders, which have to
do with money, and assault and battery
crimes in which theft is a motive. Money
is a very significant reason for people being in jail. Maybe one way of stating it is

that their aspiration for money and their ability to accumulate it are radically different. People who commit a crime often reach a state where they want money so badly that they are willing to take a higher risk than most other people are. In my opinion, a person who gets caught stealing money from a bank or a grocery store is a person who has a fantasy about what money can do for him. I find it hard to understand how someone can hold up a bank or a grocery store simply because he is hungry. I myself and many of my friends have survived hunger for long periods of time without finding it necessary to harm or threaten other people. Many people in the world live at a subsistence level that is only a fraction of that which most Americans in jail have ever lived at. Again, it is hard to believe that what a con considers to be a "subsistence level" is worth stealing to maintain, or that his need to steal in order to maintain it is in any way related to reality. Money is clearly a nightmare for those who are in jail as a result of money-related problems.

Many marriages and divorces are obviously related to money and to what it does to people who try to work out some mutual arrangement for it. Most lawyers can testify to horror stories of what money can do to heirs and heiresses and of how they can destroy whole family structures in trying to get a piece of it for themselves.

COMMENTARY ON THE FOURTH LAW

If you pick up a starving dog and make him prosperous, he will not bite you. This is the principal difference between a dog and a man.

—MARK TWAIN,
Pudd'nhead Wilson's Calendar

Barbara, my secretary, dislikes my explanation of the Fourth Law—that money is a nightmare—because I describe prisoners as examples of this nightmare. Barbara spent many years in prison. And yet, her case is an explicit example of how prisoners live out a money-related nightmare. Here is a woman who was in jail several years, from age 16 to 24. She went to jail because she was rebellious and defiant, but today, in her forties, she is one of the most conservative people I know—financially and politically. At some point she decided she was never going back to jail, and from that day on she worked hard and saved her money and obeyed almost every Ben Franklin discipline. Barbara reacts *very* strongly to people who are ex-cons and brag about it, people who brag about how they cheat other people through money deals. She has a very finely balanced, continually operating sense of people and their ethical behavior in terms of money. I didn't know Barbara as a young woman, but her present behavior strikes me as a reaction to the money-related behavior she encountered in jail.

My friend Salli feels that there is an element of condescension in the phrase, "Many of my friends have survived hunger for long periods of time without finding it necessary to harm or threaten other people." Her point is a little harder for me to deal with, because what she is saying is, "Michael, don't you take into consideration the fact that some of these cons have never realized that their grasp of reality was going to end them up in jail—or that their perceptions were wrong at all? In other words, they are trapped with a view of reality that has no built-in corrections. Their friends have the same views that they do and their parents have the same views, so they have no possible way to judge other reality perceptions."

My answer is reflected by the following

chain of thought. All societies have deviant parts of their populations, and they are deviant for certain reasons. One major category of deviance in our society has to do with that part of the population which cannot deal with our cohesive tie, the unwritten laws, which have to do with money. Biological selection (survival of the fittest) operates in the same way. The money-deviance-jail process is the cultural equivalent of the biological selection process.

When I talk about a child that dies at two years old because of malfunctioning kidneys or an infant that dies three hours after birth because of heart failure, I don't expect people to regard this as a moral judgment. There's a survival-selection process operating biologically, and a certain percentage of infants who are born will die before they are two weeks old and another smaller percentage of them will die before they are three years old. It's neither a reflection on the parents nor a reflection on our culture that this happens. (It can be a measure of the development stage of the culture, and it's also a partial measure of what is happening in the evolutionary development of our species.)

The same thing applies to the people we put in a jail. This is part of the evolutionary development of the social fabric of the culture.

I am not expressing a moral judgment. I am making very clear something that many people aren't conscious of: among the people we punish, the people we have to take out of society, 80% or more are people who are unable to deal with money. There's no emphasis on that in criminology, and when the president talks about harsh penalties as an answer to rising crime rates, he doesn't mention peoples' inability to deal with money. When over-zealous liberals talk about the conditions that breed crime in the ghettos, they speak of pouring money in to give people nice houses, thinking that will solve the problems. Just from reading the first part of the First Law it should be clear that this is misleading. Most crime has something to do with the person's own conceptions about money, what he feels he's "entitled to" or "deserves" in contrast to what he's capable of getting. When this contrast is too great, when a person's desires and wishes are significantly different from his capabilities and skills, there's going to emerge a behavior pattern that will be punished by the society.

Money is also a nightmare when looked at from the opposite perspective — from the point of view of people who have inherited a lot of money.

The Western dream is to have a lot of money, and then you can lead a life of leisure and happiness. Nothing in my experience could be further from the truth.

A friend of mine, Debbi, lives in Dallas, a very attractive young heiress who inherited a substantial amount of money from an oil fortune. She is an extremely sensitive woman, delicate, understanding, tender, and just miserable. As unhappy as she can be. She went to a fine school and she has a good education, but she can't even find a job that's meaningful. She lives in a nice apartment. She wants to associate with important people and she has enough money to do so, but she is hesitant about being friendly with people because she is afraid of being used by them.

Debbi doesn't have any clear idea of what to do with her life. She had all that money given to her at a point where she had never had a chance to find out what her life meant and what her reasons for existence were. Every day she goes out and looks for jobs and talks to people, and every night she goes home alone. Debbi never has to worry where her meals are coming from or where the rent's going to come from, but she must always be in constant terror that anybody who gets to know her will find out she has money and will use her. And that terror contributes only a small part to the lack in her existence of any sense of what she can do to become more of a person. There's always the feeling in her "Well, look, if I can't do it easily maybe I should just hire somebody else to do it for me." There are none of life's uncertainties, not much of give and take. "Why did fate choose me? Why do I have money when other people don't?" She moans. It's what Norman Mailer calls the Bryn Mawr syndrome. It's the Bryn Mawr graduate who commits suicide because the rest of the world is suffering.

Debbi inevitably has to ask herself the question "Why am I so well off? What have I done when there are all these other people I know, and respect, who have to struggle?" This guilt, this lack of understanding, this sense of responsibility for her money and not knowing how to use it to relieve other people's suffering and, most of all, her own, leads her to deep remorse. When she gives money away people become lecherous and latch on to her and won't let her go. They want more. She is merely reticent, but people treat her as if she were shy, and some are even unwilling to look at her as a person. She's in a rut, in a bind. If most people knew her well they would come to doubt that an inheritance is something beneficial.

Let me tell you about another well-to-do woman, Gina. Gina had received a substantial grant because of her involvement in the new schools movement, an area she had shown some interest in but in which she wasn't particularly active. Up to that point in her life she had been able to cope. She had a child, a husband, and played tennis. From the time she got the grant (which meant that she was expected to "do something," though nothing was specified), until the present she has been in a state of near desperation. She has been spending the money on therapy and on counseling of many types. Her nuclear family is beginning to disintegrate and she has had an emotional collapse on several occasions. Why? Because she was forced to ask herself, now that she had been given money with expectations attached "Who am I? What am I capable of doing? Why am I different in that I was given this grant and other people weren't?" These questions totally paralyzed her. She was never able to resolve them, and the stress has increased, although I am sure that in time they will be resolved. Gina's case is a beautiful example of the fact that getting money can be a nightmare.

Part of the reason why receiving money that is not a result of your own efforts is such a curse has to do with Laws Five and Six. That is because the donor, the person who gave it to you, has some implicit expectations of you, and it's impossible for you to live up to them, often because they are expectations that are not within your life experience. In the case of Debbi, the woman in Dallas, let's just presume that the grandfather who left her his money did so because he wanted to fulfill his desire to make his family like the Rothschilds—to have money and power for a long time—and because he wanted to justify his own accumulation of money. He needed to feel that his own life was justifiable, by the way he passed his money on. Now if he had asked his granddaughter point blank to live a life that he felt would have justified his accumulation of large sums of money or justified his desire to create a family like the

Rothschilds, there would have been no way that Debbi could have accepted that responsibility. However, he didn't ask her point blank but instead tried to manipulate her by leaving his money to her instead of giving it to charity. Debbi exists without realizing that when she accepted her inheritance she accepted an implicit agreement with her deceased benefactor. Even if she could recognize the bind she is in she wouldn't be able to carry out her grandfather's wishes; if she did it wouldn't be her life but his fantasy of what her life should be.

This is not unrelated to the discussion under the First Law of what happens to some artists when they are too well rewarded for their work. Like the heir who can no longer look clearly at himself or herself, the successful young artist is stuck in a rut with his existing art form, and the rewards he gets for it keep him from being able to develop further.

There's another recurring nightmare that happens to millions of couples who work and save and scrape for their retirement. These people put aside their pleasures while young, amassing their money so that their retirement years can be comfortable. They sacrifice the joy of youth for an illusion of security. Many of these people come to realize too late that they have spent the bulk of their lives lusting for retirement. There must be considerable anguish in coming to this realization near the end of life. Think of their desperate attempts to have fun now that they have forgotten how. Is this not an example of money as a nightmare? (Eric Erikson claims that this crisis of old age is resolved by simply deciding that everything worked out O.K. Ha!)

A while back a woman who had grown up in a well-to-do suburban Philadelphia family came to my office. She had always been given anything she wanted and her every whim and desire had been satisfied. Why did she come to me? She wanted to start a camp where she and all her friends could hang out. She well knew she could raise the money, but what she was looking for was somebody who would actually do the work of starting and running the camp. I have seldom been so struck with a woman; she was a total sump. When we were together she drained every bit of energy that I could muster. In her life every whim was gratified, leaving her in a complete hole that drained the energy of everyone around her. In desperation, I think, she was trying to re-enact the one part of her life that had been fun—an early camping experience. The rest of her life had been stolen from her by readily-available money and the consequent lack of passions in her existence.

How does money become a nightmare for the ordinary working person? The treadmill is a common example. People work hard to provide themselves and their families with worldly goods, new and better toys, better appliances. It's the something we joke about so often—keeping up with the Joneses. Yet the process of working for more money so consumes our time and is considered so valid by our peers that we never stop to examine our values, our priorities. Even when people carry the Protestant work ethic to extremes we never question what they are doing. I'll elaborate a little; after all this *does* include most of us.

A man came into my office in desperate need of a loan. He was working fanatically on a business venture—one that was not a bad idea but which was obviously not immediately feasible; it would take from five to ten years to accomplish. He thought he had gotten promises from the Bank of America and American Express for help on his idea, but I knew from my experience with these companies that what they had really said was "If you get this, this, and this, then come back to see us and we'll take a more careful look." He had gotten dozens of corporations strung out with his idea and gotten that sort of nebulous promise. Each time a corporation said "Great" the prospect of imminent success got closer in his mind. He was living a fantasy. He was borrowing extensively and was enormously in debt. He had told only his wife about the financial strait that he was in; he had not told his children, nor did any of his friends and neighbors know to what extent his ambition had taken him. He scheduled meetings just before noon so he could be taken out to lunch and thus save money. He stayed up late at night so his children wouldn't see him starching and ironing his own shirts because he could no longer afford to send them to a laundry.

Since almost no answer I could give him would have been much less painful, I told him frankly that bankruptcy was a perfectly sound answer to his problems. I wanted him to realize that if he ever faced the fact that he *could* go through bankruptcy most of the people to whom he was in debt would probably accept him as a realistic person and allow him to work out his debt without actually having to go into bankruptcy. I felt that he would probably find that his children would support him completely and that they would be willing to give up an awful lot to help, as would his wife and his friends. He didn't have to drive a fancy car and look like a successful businessman in order to work on his idea. I felt he should look at all the things he valued and cherished and realize the pain he created for himself because he had placed money goals above family values. He had created a nightmare, and he was in incredible pain.

Money nightmares can arise out of the simplest relationships between people.

Since I've been on the Board of POINT, I have had four or five bitter attacks directed at me, because I have access to money. One woman took me to lunch and proceeded to bawl me out because I hadn't given her money for her project, which she felt was obviously the most important thing in the world. She was furious that I was giving grants to other projects and not to hers. Now the fact that that hurt me in some way is my own fault. The reason I was hurt was because up to that point she had been a close friend, and now she was literally saying that my behavior in making grants to projects that appealed to me was causing her pain. I knew this was not true, but the lunch was agony.

At one point a community warehouse group that had been operating for a year wanted me to give them money. I'd considered giving a grant, but I felt the idea had low priority and my intuition said no.

One night I visited them, and when I sat down three people told me how terrible I was for not giving them any money. These were ordinary human beings; you'd probably love them. But because their project was so important to them and I was in a position of having money available as a foundation donor I was treated viciously. Their main argument was that if I was a friend why shouldn't I be willing to help them out with money? I tried to point out to them that the sad thing to me was that people failed to realize they saw me only as a source of money and not as a human being capable of giving them other help, of working with them in any other capacity except as a donor of money. I have a lot of skills for helping people get projects under way, and the thing that was the most painful in this case, and in several other cases, was the fact that some of my so-called friends saw me only as a source of money and not as a broader human being. I felt just the way my heiress friend feels.

How do you keep money from being a nightmare? How do you deal with money nightmares in the first place?

Probably my answer would be a dose of the first three Laws:

First, recognize that the values in your life have to be powerful, tangible values that exist independently of money.

Second, you must realize that there are underlying relationships between you and the world around you. These should be reflected in your behavior in dealing with money—all the way from keeping books to being honest with yourself about your monetary perceptions.

Third, you should recognize, hopefully with a sense of humor, that money is a dream, that it's absolutely fantasy-like. When at any point you begin to substitute money as a goal, as a motivating factor, for the more important things in your life, you may end up in pain. And "nightmare," the Fourth Law, comes about as a consequence of violating the first three Laws.

Lolly. I am a twenty-nine-year-old woman with about $200,000 in personal assets, which yield an annual income of around $10,000. I also have about $5,000 in annual income from trusts I don't control. I have never been married. And I didn't earn my assets except by being born into the right circumstances.

This fact is difficult to say flat out. Few people know about it. I prefer it that way. Which is not to say that my money isn't riding around in front of me but instead that I want to control that particular bit of information.

I am afraid, I suppose, of being considered rich, a word which I do not use about myself even to myself. In some of the places I've been the fact that I have money would set me apart, would create

envy and resentment and might well set
me up for a hustle. In other places I might
be thought of as pleasant enough but not
worth even considering as a rich person.
I have enough money to experience some
of its disadvantages, but not enough to
allow me to be particularly extravagant,
at least not more than once. I like
money: having it, making it, and sometimes spending it. But it does affect me.
And just as I can't keep amounts completely straight I have trouble being en-
tirely clear about its effect.

What I am clear about is:

1. I want to hang on to my money. I have
   been called tight-fisted. I want to
   make or have more of it, but not necessarily a lot more.
2. Not only do I want to hang on to
   money, I'm also quite attached to it. I
   have heard that we only have the use
   of money during our lifetimes but that
   it is not "ours." The stuff I have sure

feels like mine; I don't feel particularly free about its coming and going.

3. Money does, however, buy me a kind of freedom. A freedom to thumb my nose at people who would try to pressure me economically if I became too threatening to them. And a freedom to find out what I want to do, because at times I can do and have done absolutely nothing. Those freedoms can send me way up or down: they can make me exhilarated or heavy with what a Peanuts cartoon called "the burden of a great potential."

4. I do not want to expend a lot of energy on money.

5. I do not like to talk about money unless I know someone fairly well. But then when I start I sometimes won't stop.

6. I have a rather strong conviction that I'm special, different, a cut above the other people—not that I like myself

any better than the average mildly masochistic American likes himself. Although I'm ashamed of the times I have been snobbish, I am definitely a snob. The horror that I have when I see myself as being like everyone else has a lot to do, I suspect, with my money.

7. I do not like ostentation, although I can forgive it more easily in those who don't have money than in those who do.

I have wondered where I'd be without money. Actually, I have an idea. For the first five years after college I worked. At that point I had about $2,000 a year in "unearned" income, which I only used once. The nest egg was there, but I lived on what I earned. I let my jobs define me; I was ambitious in a career way, although I hated the word career. I always assumed that I would work after college at least until I got married, which I never did.

Although I knew I could fall back on my parents if I really needed to, I assumed I wouldn't. My father says he values his children's independence. I was and still am proud of mine.

The direction I chose to go in led me to programs which aided the poor and the blacks. This may have been a sort of "noblesse oblige," although I hope not. It may have been a channel for me to express a personal anger in the milieu of the justifiable anger of the oppressed. It may have been wanting to save the world instead of myself, or, most likely, wanting to be useful and helpful. In spite of the bad name "doing good" has gotten, I, like a lot of other people, want to do good — to do something that will make a difference. Whatever the motivation, the jobs gave me an education about some facts of life that money had sheltered me from. I do not, for example, romanticize or even like poverty, for myself or anyone else.

People who have money often think that it is the fault of poor people that they are poor. I would say it is probably more our fault: "our" in this instance meaning the haves. I also found that people *are* people; money isn't everything, but that's easier to say when you have it.

I have felt a conflict when working with or talking to people who have much less money than I do, a reaction felt by any reasonably sensitive American traveling in a very poor area. I am aware of the huge difference between the way I spend a dollar and the way some others have to scrape to earn it. I am also, of course, aware of the resentment I create. In fact, I can understand, although I don't condone, the isolation of richer people from much poorer people.

But the discomfort does not come merely from a fear of being disliked, nor just from a feeling of guilt about having more money, but from an unwillingness to part with much of it. The problem, obviously, would not exist if I were to give all my money away. I don't, because I know it wouldn't make any difference. I also don't because I don't want to.

What I have concluded about the guilt/responsibility question is that my money is one fact of my existence. I had nothing to do with its being given to me. Nothing. Nor did I have anything to do with how the money came into being. But every time the abuse of a river, a tree, a customer, or an employee puts money in my pocket, I too am a culprit. The people who make the decisions of whether or not to pollute, cheat and discriminate say they do so in my name. I have tried to research some of the "social costs" of the money sources and present the information to other members of my family who might be able to do something. I am still continuing this effort, although I'm not satisfied with the results.

My sense of family, which is strong, has to do with relatives whom I know or have known. Although there are lots of relatives I don't particularly like, both sides of my family are quite family minded. Because enough relatives have had genealogical streaks, I can trace my family back pretty far. But I don't have any sense of pedigree, for a good reason; I come from a typically American mishmash. None the less, in societal terms, I am somewhat statusy, although the status of WASPy types has slipped in recent years.

My friends don't fit any particular pattern, but some of the men I've been with, especially in the last few years, have been less "statusy": Jews and blacks. I am not sure how to evaluate that—whether money has anything to do with it or if it's a function of the things I'm interested in. I do feel a little uncomfortable writing about status, me, and men; probably I see some sort of societally determined difference between me and them, and I probably have some residual prejudices. By other criteria, the men I have known have been as smart, wise, or sophisticated as I am—or more so. In any case, I think I've spent time with some pretty good people. Actually, I have a problem making any unqualified generalizations about the men I've been with, although I put a lot of energy into my relationships with men, usually with one man but never with him exclusively. And about 75% of the time it's the man who ends the relationship, status or no status.

One example of my money muddying things up with men is my fear that men might want me for my money. I've heard enough stories about hunting for a rich wife to make me wary. Actually, it's a question of degree; I don't have enough money to make it worth someone's while if he doesn't like me, and I've been dumped enough times to know that the money doesn't make that much difference. But I never know how much difference it does make. When the thought does enter my head it's an ugly one. It makes me suspicious and tight. It is, after all, a bummer to think that someone, especially a man, wants to be with me, to whatever degree, not because of me but because of my money. On the other hand, I, too, would just as soon spend my time with someone who has lots of money.

The reactions of men to my having money have varied from "I'd like to have it" to "Sure, it's attractive" to "I don't give a shit" to "I don't particularly envy you" to "It's an unattractive aspect of you" to anger at my prejudices.

I have also been told that I have ways of letting people know my situation. I've even caught myself at it.

I feel bad sometimes when people I

know have money problems, especially
the insoluble kind. I can see how the
need for money can dull or destroy. A
need for money which I would call exces-
sive is making one man I know selfish,
manipulative, and limited.

My current "honey" and I had a big
discussion recently about my money and
his feelings about it. We've had several
other discussions: my feelings about my
money, his feelings about money. He ac-
cuses me of class snobbism (some of
which I admit to); I accuse him of class
snobbism (some of which he admits to).
This particular discussion came up because of a family discussion about how
much money there was and what might
happen to it. Although I generally have a
hard time not blabbing about what's on
my mind at any given moment, I was reluctant to get into it. I was afraid he'd
like me less if he knew there might be less
money. He had implied it before, and I

suspected that he was interested in my money. When he finally got me to admit that I was asking if he was after my money, he answered yes. He said that to him my money was one of the attractive things about me. Yes, he wouldn't mind spending or having some of it. I asked him if my money made him act any differently toward me than he would otherwise. He said no. If money does stop him from being hostile, annoying or cold at times, it's not noticeable. He has said that I don't have enough money (but until he reads this, he doesn't know exactly how much there is) and that money by itself is not enough to interest him in anybody. On the other hand I can't help being suspicious—especially because his close friends tend to be rich. One new wrinkle since our discussion: when it seems he's being gratuitously unpleasant I wonder if it's because I told him he would never have any control over my money.

I should say about this particular friend that I think he is right: on balance money isn't that important a factor between us. It's there, but lots of other things outrank it.

A more recent postscript: He decided that he didn't want to marry me after all. The irony is that now I'm a little less suspicious of him.

Some thoughts I couldn't fit in anywhere else:

My money is like a big pillow or a soft blanket to fall back on or to wrap up in when I'm feeling low. Periodically, I get into moods during which I make desperate attempts to reach out and/or pull into myself. When one of these gets bad and my fantasies get more and more catatonic, I feel that I could just stay right here in my house forever. The truth is: I could. Now I have a job, so the current likelihood is that I wouldn't hole up in the house, but for several years I had absolutely no responsibilities. I am still too close to the years when I didn't have a full time job to be able to analyze, catalogue, and file them away. I do know that I was lonely then and am still lonely now, and continually plagued by the questions about the purpose of my existence. I realize that money does not have a monopoly on or even cause these questions. My money may have exacerbated such problems, because I do not *have* to go out. I can afford to isolate myself.

The distribution of wealth in this country is such that many people just don't have enough. Because of this people who have money are hated for having it, especially if we don't give it away, or are hassled if we do give it away. Part of the job I now have involves fund raising. Perhaps another irony. I hear people say things like "I don't give a shit about her; I just want her money," and I hear of resentment against "coupon clippers." I cringe somewhere inside.

Someone suggested that my money was destructive because I was rewarded for the wrong thing. I don't think it's so much a question of the wrong thing; I think everyone should be rewarded for being. But I have not earned my money, and to most Americans unearned goodies are akin to sin.

YOU CAN NEVER REALLY GIVE MONEY AWAY.

COMMENTARY ON
THE FIFTH LAW

I GUESS THIS law sounds bizarre on the face of it. Maybe I didn't realize how other people would interpret it when I wrote it. My friend Salli reacted by saying that she thought it was because there's so much of it around. That's not really my view. I prefer to see money as a flow that can be seen in static or dynamic terms. In dynamic terms, money describes a relationship: borrower/lender, or seller/buyer, or parent/child. Looked at over a period of time, money flows in certain channels, like electricity though wires. The wires define the relationship, and the flow is the significant thing to look at. The Fifth Law comes from looking at money in this dynamic sense. We are used to seeing it in static terms, where we normally expect to see a two-directional flow associated with money. For example, I give the man behind the counter $50 and he rents me a Cessna 172 airplane to fly for an hour. We *expect* the two-directional flow, the exchange. Then we see someone who gives a friend $25.00 and says "keep it." We call that a "gift" because it is a one-directional flow, or at least it seems to be, in the context of a short period of time. The Fifth Law of Money suggests that by looking at the gift in a larger or longer term of perspective we will see that it is part of a two-way flow.

Dick Raymond likes the term "alliance" to describe the giving relationship. I think a lot of people can identify with that term. I feel more comfortable with the words "loan" or "investment" to describe the giving relationship. From a casual perspective, the lender gives the money and the borrower just signs a piece of paper. In a real-life giving situation, the piece of paper (loan note) and its contents are implicit in the situation but are not customarily talked about in our culture.

Many of these concepts have come out of my experiences in foundation work, over the years, during which time I've given away over hundreds of thousands of dollars. Just saying that appalls me, because I can't even remember where most of the money went without systematically searching my mind or records. That sum of money sounds startling to me; I had probably never given away more than $5,000 to charity in my whole sweet life. In the case of the money, I spent an inordinate number of hours thinking about the problem of giving and being very emotionally involved in the process.

When I think of my good grants and bad grants, the bad ones that come to mind relate to situations where I gave money to someone or some project which appealed to me on an intellectual level but was not emotionally satisfying—something for which I didn't feel any passion and in which I was not involved. Conceptually, these were giving situations where the flow was one way, the loan was not repaid. Repayment, of course, was to be in emotional satisfaction.

One such grant was to a woman who headed her own organization. She made a spectacular initial impression on me because of her forthrightness and her outspokenness on corporate social responsibility. When I learned that she needed money for air fare to enable her to attend and speak out at a corporation's annual meeting, I provided the money. As it turned out, (1) I was not around to attend the meeting, and (2) she sent someone in her place. The outcome of the

158 · *The Seven Laws of Money*

meeting was merely a little PR in the newspaper. Although I'm sure that dollar for dollar it was as useful to society as some comparable projects, I nevertheless felt pretty bad about the grant.

Later on, the more I got to know her, the more I found her to be a physically cold woman whom I could not feel very close to. As a consequence, I resolved that I wasn't going to give money to anybody whom I didn't feel emotionally strong and warm about, and that I wasn't going to give money when I couldn't be involved in the project.

The board of POINT made several other bad grants from our point of view. One was to an individual who received a grant to work on feminists' issues and then never did a thing. Both the board and she had far greater expectations of her abilities than it was possible for her to meet— which brought her close to a nervous breakdown. In a similar situation, an-

other woman found the sensible solution
and gave her grant back.

One of the interesting lessons Stewart
Brand (who is also a POINT board member) learned is that you don't give money
to an idea. One of his worst grants was
when he picked an idea rather than the
person who was to carry out the idea. The
idea was that a poor, fairly effective man
could be made very effective by giving
money to help him. He gave a $15,000
grant to a man who usually lived on
$5,000 a year. The grant was blown in six
months, and nothing happened; the guy
just went back to looking for a job. In this
case nothing happened. The money
changed hands—it was all seen as a one-
way transaction by Stewart and his
grantee. Stewart ended up with the pain
of having made a poor grant.

Some of my very best grants have been
made using Dick Raymond's concept of
"alliance." One grant was to Alice Tepper
Marlin, of the Council on Economic Pri-

orities. Because of Alice's qualities and a close working relationship with her a number of good projects came out of our association. The grant to a strong individual *plus* the relationship was effective, powerful, and rewarding to all of us. Even after the end of the grant year Alice still hadn't used the full amount of her grant.

I don't wish to give the impression that POINT grants are calculated like loan agreements. As we've gone along, I've learned the emotional components of the giving business and have tried to keep the consequences out in the open. This openness is different from the policy of the traditional foundation, where there is often a secret string attached to grants. Without being open about it the traditional foundation has something specific that it wants done, and when it makes a grant, unless progress is made toward its unstated goals, the grant recipient is slowly tortured. What happens is that the grantee's ability to get more funds depends on how closely his project conforms to the Foundation's hidden agenda. Grants are usually renewable annually, and only in rare instances are they given for periods in excess of a year. The whole grant renewal concept is very much like the way a bank makes loans. Most bank commercial loans are only for 90 days. Banks always want the option of getting their money back if they are not satisfied with the way in which the borrower is operating. Doesn't granting sound like lending?

It has also been my experience in foundation work that the traditional foundation operates on the same basis that I do in terms of emotional components, without being open about it. Virtually all their grants go to people whom they already know and like—even when the actual grant is made in the name of an institution. I'd say POINT's most successful approach to money giving has been the open recognition that we are creating alliances with *people*. Out of our alliances we have developed some mutual goals without setting arbitrary criteria and objectives. We find our growth is therefore spontaneous—*not* as a result of money but as a result of our associations.

Ted McIlvenna and Lew Durham, two brilliant men who had a great deal of responsibility for establishing Glide Foundation in San Francisco, have long been aware that their most successful grants have been to individuals or to small groups of closely-knit associates.

One of their guiding concepts in the creation of Glide was that one of the most effective operatives in a society is not a person acting on his own, but one who has the continued support and interaction with colleagues. This collective approach parallels the concept of an alliance; money is not given away—an alliance is created.

Being put on the Board of POINT was a gift to me. I have viewed it as a two-way flow; my acceptance of the "responsibility" is my repayment. I have always kept in mind that the money came from *The Last Whole Earth Catalog* and that in some distinct sense its use is related to its origin. The origins of the money and the experiences with it have heavily influenced many Board members, particularly me.

The fund of one hundred sixty thousand dollars for completely discretionary personal grants, available to each board member, has caused me to re-evaluate and restructure my life. For the last two years I have been conscious of what my energy and money are supporting. I've had to decide what I consider to be most important—what my passions are, why I am alive and what I am going to do with the rest of my life. The questions could have been posed in an abstract way before I started, but the actual acceptance of responsibility for having the money forced me to answer the question and struggle with the outcome.

I accepted a responsibility when I accepted the money. I now am discovering what are the most effective things I can be doing to influence the world around me (or to influence *me*, which is another way of looking at it). In the process, I have had to modify my perceptions to the point where I can say I am satisfied with the validity of my image of the world. I have come to know that my image is stable enough and that it is clear enough to me, so that I can draw some conclusions about how my behavior will affect my surroundings.

I put part of this in writing, in the form of a memo to all POINT Board members submitted as part of the POINT records. The rest was in the form of changes in my life.

The not so obvious part of the struggle dealt with overcoming roadblocks: two were mentioned in the Third Law—the sign written in the desert with a tractor and the sex furniture that I had built. Doing this overcame my mental roadblocks, sort of opened the closed loops in my mind that had focused my energy on minor fantasy-like things in such a way that I couldn't get on to the major things.

I have to admit that the availability of money simply forced the issues, forced me to deal with the fact that I had to take on the small projects that I had emotionally committed myself to, as well as the large ones.

In daily life, it's not that different. There are a lot of things I have to do during the week, some pleasant, some unpleasant, some large, some small. Often the small, unpleasant ones are so obvious they keep me from doing the rest. Then I get a feeling of guilt from not doing the rest and I become depressed. I have slowly learned, after all these years of having to deal with this problem, that I have to change my behavior to the extent that I complete the unpleasant, small tasks with a determination that allows me to go on then to the other jobs. Otherwise, nothing will happen.

An analogy that Salli just came up with is perfect — if you don't do the dishes after each meal you finally end up having to do a huge pile of dishes that have stacked up.

Before ending this chapter on giving it might be interesting to mention that I got to thinking about "allowances" for children while writing this. When I was doing research in the Library of Congress I looked for money-and-children books and books on the subject of allowances. There was only one writer who had touched on the subject, and she had narrow perspectives with a great deal of vintage-1940 psychological advice. And yet allowances are damned important. They are given with the intention of shaping a child's personality, and they carry with them very strong implicit messages and expectations.

Just checking around my own neighborhood and asking the friends of my three children about their allowances I found a wide range of patterns. One family doesn't give allowances, but gives the kids large sums of money on birthdays and holidays. Another family gives the children large allowances, but also a list of "approved" items it can be spent on. Still another family ties the allowances to specific chores around the house; the more chores the more money. Some allowances are given just because the child exists; some are given out of guilt; some to teach money handling; some to encourage responsibility for money; and some just to have another last-resort punishment, "I'll cut off your allowance." But, interestingly, I don't find much self-examination on our part as to what this parent-child-money relationship is.

Giving? The Fifth Law probably should be applied in our own homes first.

Foundations Gone Wild. An example of foundations gone wild occurred recently.

I funded Margo St. James to organize a prostitutes' collective to protect street prostitutes from the inhuman daily abuse they get from the police, the courts, and hypocrites. I advised her to let a few local foundations know what she was up to so they would be aware of her project if in the future she should need to go to them for funds. I read the letter she sent to them; no request, just a friendly letter saying what she was doing. One liberal foundation, Pacific Change, invited her over for lunch and grilled her cruelly and mercilessly the same way they do groups they regularly screen. They berated her for not being serious, not being a member of a minority and not being poor enough. Fortunately, she told them to go to hell and left. Another foundation simply sent her a letter of rejection, although she hadn't applied for money. These institutions are examples of how most foundations are so structured that they become numb in the process of dealing with the pain people feel in the donor/grantee relationship.

YOU CAN NEVER REALLY RECEIVE MONEY AS A GIFT.

MONEY IS EITHER borrowed or lent or possibly invested. It is never given or received without those concepts implicit in it. Some people may say "Oh! I understand that, what you are really giving is karma or receiving is karma and karma can be good or bad." Well, that's a possible interpretation. What I interpret this to mean is that the act or supposed act of giving money implies the creation of a "relationship"; It's a temporary imbalance. Giving money requires some repayment, if it's not repaid the nightmare elements enter into it.

Foundations learn that the kind of people who write good proposals and go asking for money are frequently the people who are incapable of doing anything once they have it; they are good askers, maybe because they don't understand what goes along with the money that is given to them, and the responsibilities. Maybe the Hope Diamond is an example of what giving things away is all about. I see many written foundation proposals from many different kinds of people over a long period of time. In my view, most of these people really ought to examine themselves. It seems that they become proposal writers and in the process of getting grants they become fictitious, imaginary people themselves. The process is highly destructive to them. Many people I know who have a great deal of money and have tried to give it away have found that it can't be done, that it creates as much of a burden to give it away as it does to keep it and that it is virtually impossible to give away because of the impact it has on the personality of the person doing the giving.

Not too long ago a group came to me and wanted to buy a gigantic piece of land. It was a group oriented around an Eastern religion and they naturally wanted to raise *money* for the gigantic piece of land. I said "You don't want money, you want supporters. You can go out and look for supporters and in the process ask for money, but don't forget what you're really after. Supporters." They did this. They contacted countless people, always asking for a small amount of money but in the process realizing that the commitment of a small amount of money was a commitment of support. And, of course, it was the support that built the institution and helped it grow. The institution is still growing. If this religious group had gotten a grant in the beginning it probably would have blown their whole future. Where would their supporters and friends and energy have come from, especially when the grants and funds began to run out in two or three years?

Remember the Second Law, which also applies to Law Six. When you get money, you've got to follow the Second Law, and you must deliver something for it. A gift of money is really a contract; it's really a repayable loan, and it requires performance and an accounting of performance that is satisfactory to the giver.

There are many ways in which the gift of money is not a gift at all, of course. It does destroy people's lives, as has happened to some Indian groups. I know of a free clinic that had done a spectacularly good job in San Francisco. It applied for a grant and was given an enormous sum of money. It virtually went out of business three weeks later as the whole group squabbled over what to do with the money and how to use it.

COMMENTARY ON THE SIXTH LAW

This Law sounds fairly harsh, but it is no more than the converse of the Fifth Law and embodies the same concepts of a loan, an alliance, and the long-term dynamic view of money.

There is a slight difference between the Fifth and Sixth Laws, just as there is a difference between a so-called giver and a receiver. The receiver plays more of a passive role and, like the heiress described earlier, the giver's action occasionally imposes a need for defensive reaction on the part of the receiver. Certainly such was the case for the woman in the Fifth Law who gave back her grant.

To some extent, thinking as I write about this vulnerability of the receiver

and situations such as Lolly's generates a
feeling of despair in me. Thinking about
money, and money itself, has the power
to evoke despair. Receiving money and
the whole potential for despair in relation
to money is the subject of this chapter.

Several years ago my father forwarded
to me my share of an inheritance from a
great uncle (Abraham Lincoln Phillips, a
Shakespearian ham turned retail clothier
who spent most of his 95 years in Peta-
luma, California, where my father's family settled in the 1850s.) My share was
$500 after the inheritance was divided
among my three younger brothers and
me. I wrote my father and asked if he
knew of any explicit or implicit expectations that my great uncle had concerning
the money. My father took me seriously
and remembered what his uncle used to
jokingly tell him when he gave gifts of
spending money: "Use it to pay the mortgage." That's exactly what I did with it. I

was lucky; I knew the Sixth Law and acted decisively to find out the history of the money. If I hadn't had this background information I would have had to think seriously about what to do with the money, and the process of thinking about it could have been painful and revealing about myself, since it would have led me to deal with the money/despair issue openly. I would have had to choose between saving it or spending it on some possession. Saving would have led me to examine the question of why I save and what kind of protective money shield I was creating—protection from what? If instead I spent the money on a product, I would wonder who I needed to impress, what new need was I fabricating, and why? What kind of life-style was I driving at?

All these questions would have been generated by a gift of money. Money the psychiatrist? Yes, in a way. I see money as a mirror. An examination of your money and the way you use money is a way of understanding yourself in the same way that a mirror provides a way of seeing yourself. But, of course, because of the monsters that Freud found hiding within us we can be frightened, paralyzed and mortified by the mirror of money. It is commonly said that money is the root of all evil. This is a misphrasing of the original biblical translation "the *love* of money is the root of all evil." But who's to quibble when the mirror is such an easy thing to blame for what it reveals?

The monster/mirror quality of money became apparent to me a while back when I had a chance to see it in comparison to sex, a subject that clearly has intensity, fear and repression associated with it. For six months I was in a discussion group with eight men, counterpart to the women's consciousness groups. Once during those six months we brought up the subject of money and once we brought up the subject of homosexuality. In my own mind I know with certainty that the male fear of homosexuality is one of the most powerful cultural forces that influence our daily lives and our views of sexuality—yet it was so emotionally charged that we discussed it only for about an hour and politely went on to other subjects. Most of us felt we covered the subject adequately. Money we covered in only half an hour. Everyone politely described "the depths of his feelings" about money, and that was it. It's a subject so charged up that *we are often not conscious that we are not discussing it.*

I have strong feelings associated with money that have emerged in writing this book. I keep asking myself as I write why some of my dealings with money have been so painful. You probably don't feel the same pain and agony while you're reading this. As I sit here writing, the pain takes the form of a personal depression that comes from saying "Help! What in the world is there for me to do? I'm worthless." It's the kind of depression that just sits there and stares at you—a sort of a gloom that implies there's a big hole inside of you, while you just sit and feel that enormous hole. Maybe it's like looking at your leg when you know it's about to be amputated; it embodies hopes on the one hand and memories on the other. I see the immediate present as some sort of transition which doesn't give me any confidence or feeling of security. Talking about the elements of money and examining them creates the feeling that money is tied to the whole universe. Maybe my feelings arise because we don't have the rituals surrounding money or writing about money that we have intertwined with religion, for example—rituals which allow us to deal with powerful forces and to derive some of the excite-

ment, joy and ecstasy that come with rituals when they are applied to strong
forces. Maybe the pain comes from writing about money, which is a non-logical,
non-rational subject to begin with—
money being experiential, almost hyper-
experiential. Money governs experiences,
yet it can't be experienced itself. In that
sense it's like art. You can experience a
painting directly by seeing it, but the
"creative process" behind the painting is
something the viewer can't experience.

Guilt plays an extremely powerful role
in our relations to money. There are large
numbers of people who feel that they
have too much money, there are many
who feel that "other people" have too
much money, and there are many who
sometimes feel that they have devoted too
much of their lives to seeking money.
This is a reflection of guilt and money.

Guilt also plays an important role in
many forms of giving and consequently in

receiving. Of all the forms of charity, direct giving provides a good example of guilt (like giving to the Red Cross for food packages, giving aid to victims of an earthquake or to women who are the victims of rape after a revolution.) When giving is direct and deals with personal guilt, people pour the money out. Their feelings of guilt are sometimes of such a quality that enormous quantities of useless material are amassed. Almost every time there's a disaster people bring their food and clothing to the Red Cross, and usually the Red Cross can't do a thing with them. It would cost much more to ship used clothes and dented food cans to victims of a disaster (who usually don't wear our kind of clothes and don't eat our kind of food) than it would cost to buy the equivalent items in an adjacent country. And yet the food and clothing pour in.

THERE ARE WORLDS WITHOUT MONEY.

I THINK IT'S important to keep in mind that there are possible worlds without money. When you're asleep and dreaming, that's a world without money. There may be other places in the universe, there may be other concepts and other states of life in which there's no money, but the last Law makes it really hard to forget that everything we do when we're awake is related to money. You can take it away, such as with people in prisoner of war camps; but cigarettes become money. It's there as long as there are people to interact and they are awake.

COMMENTARY ON THE SEVENTH LAW

This law has a little ironic twist to it, because what it says is that the world we live in is the world of money, and those of us who aren't willing to see it and deny the role of money will unfortunately be the ones for whom the world will be the least pleasant.

The history of man's creation of money isn't too clear, but it is fascinating. I got most of my information from Rupert J. Ederer's *The Evolution of Money* and Paul Einzig's *Primitive Money*. Man has apparently been a tool-using animal for several million years, but the period around 5,000 years ago when he began to domesticate animals was the first time rings and axes appear to have been used as exchange goods. These artifacts have been found in burial sites in Brittany, Crete, Mycenae and Silesia. By the time of the Pharaohs, 4,000 years ago, copper was used as the unit of exchange in Egypt.

An alloy of copper, silver and gold was used in Babylonian, Indian, and Chinese coins. Hammurabi's code required merchants to accept silver in payment for commerce, and Egyptian granaries recorded their banking activities in the form of grain loans with interest.

A thousand years ago, the Chinese in the Tang Dynasty issued paper money, followed five hundred years ago by the development of banking and paper currency in Europe. (Curiously, the Jews seem to have been around the Middle East when coins emerged, and they were right on the scene when banking first developed in Northern Italy.)

Today money and the processes that are its visible qualities; interest, profit, capital, inflation, etc.—seem to be everywhere—in spite of the fact that there was no conference held to create it, there is no constitution to control it, and no advertising campaign carries it to the ends of the planet.

And yet the Seventh Law says that there are worlds without money. They are the worlds of art, poetry, music, dance, sex, etc., the essentials of human life. The Seventh Law should be like a star that is your guide. You know that you cannot live on the star; it is not physically a part of your life, but rather an aid to orientation. You are not going to reach this star, but in some sense neither are you going to reach your destination without it to guide you. The recognition of the role of money in your life from birth until the moment of your death comes from an understanding of where you are: it is where you walk and struggle and eat and think and understand. The star—the Seventh Law—is there to say that there is somewhere without money. You can't reach it except by focusing on the non-money parts of life—what you do, how you work, who you are, and who you associate with.

This is related to the famous statement that a fish could not discover water, or that Indians did not see "scenic vistas" as we modern tourists do. That there are worlds without money is a way of saying that a fish's life would be different if he could simply acknowledge that he does live in water, and the legendary Indian's life would have been different if he had realized that he lived in an environment that was mostly within the range of his eyesight. The star—the Seventh Law—is a way of saying that we are in the money, just as a fish is in the water, and that recognition of this can greatly influence how we respond to the world around us.

───────── EPILOGUE ─────────

A GREAT DEAL of agony is involved in writing a book, so I think it's only fair to offer the reader who might be curious an idea of why I was willing to spend the time and energy to write this book.

The history of *The Seven Laws of Money* is fairly straightforward. The original Seven Laws of Money were compiled in the form of a seven page "pamphlet" at the request of Salli Rasberry, who was working on a book concerned with free schools, called *Rasberry Exercises*. Salli wanted some information for people working in free schools to help them cope with the seemingly insurmountable problems surrounding money.

It happened that my friend Jug 'n' Candle was in town, and I mentioned to him the day before I was to be interviewed by Salli that she had asked me to talk about money. Jug, a poet, always seems to be in town when I need him. He said he'd be glad to help and proceeded to tell me about the concept of "seven laws," which comes from Tao philosophy. There are a number of sets of seven laws, like the Seven Laws of Travel and the Seven Laws of Prayer. He told me how you constructed them. He didn't lay out the whole process in advance, but instead led me to discover it. He said, "I'll tell you how to create the First Law and then you see if you can think of something about money that fits that description." I thought of it and told him. Then he told me how to create the Second Law once I had the first. I thought about it and came up with the Second Law. The Third Law was formed as a synthesis of the first two, the Fourth is its opposite, and so on.

We proceeded until I had done the Sixth Law. Then I asked Jug how to arrive at the Seventh Law. And he said "You can't arrive at it. It deals with something that you just can't arrive at." I said, "Oh, that sounds to me like—," and thereupon I laid out the Seventh Law. "Yea", he says, "That's what the Seventh Law is— that's the sort of conclusion you jump to when you realize you can't logically arrive at the Seventh Law. It's like the question that is always on the end of a French doctoral thesis."

I then had the tape transcribed, typed and sent to Salli. Along the way some of my friends got copies. One in particular was Dick Raymond, who liked it so much he made some copies and started passing them around.

Within a few months I had more than a dozen requests from people around the United States—churches in Atlanta, executives at IBM in New York, etc. asking for copies of "The Seven Laws." Eventually a major publisher, Penguin, sent its

West Coast Editor, Don Burns, with an offer of an advance to turn it into a book. I agreed to think about it, which I did. The only thing we settled on at that time was that if I offered the book to anybody it would be to Penguin, and that we would keep a record of our negotiations and discussions, which would be included in the book. (In the end Penguin's New York editors overruled Don and said no.)

As the book began to take form in my mind, a group of friends coalesced around a publishing organization called Word Wheel. My personal ties to Word Wheel went back a long way, to my membership on the Board of Portola Institute. Portola spawned *Big Rock Candy Mountain*, which published several educational journals and ultimately became Word Wheel. This made some sort of an alliance a natural thing.

It took three months for me to decide to do the book. My struggle had to do with reasons that are not necessarily obvious. I was not too interested in the money which could have come from the advance, nor fame, nor the desire to help people. My reason for not doing it in the beginning was that I had already written "The Seven Laws," and anything else seemed like it would be ineffective popularizing. Like the Sufi tale, in which the Murshid came into the classroom after the class had decided to ask him some terribly difficult question. "What is the meaning of life?" they all asked him at once, and he said "Which of you knows the answer?" No one raised his hand, so the Murshid said "In that case, you wouldn't understand if I told you." The next day the students discussed the matter and came up with a solution. When the Murshid walked in they asked him to tell what the meaning of life was, and he asked "How many of you know the answer?" They all raised their hands, and he said "In that case you certainly don't need to hear it from me." The third day they thought they really had him. He walked into the classroom and they asked him again the meaning of life. He once again asked "How many of you know the answer?" This time half the class raised their hands and the other half didn't. He said "Fine, now the half that knows can tell the half that doesn't."

Using this story as a model, I was highly reluctant to work for months to popularize what I had already done in a matter of seven pages.

Other things influenced me, however, and slowly changed my mind. There were discussions with Jug 'n' Candle which led me to think that I could possibly write a book that I would be interested in reading myself. Secondly, my mother said I should do it. She wanted a famous son. Her conception of fame was to be known within a certain elite circle of book readers, a friendly group of people to be famous among.

I was also concerned about the "fictitious quality" of books, especially nonfiction ones. This quality can be seen in analogy to a zebra. A book is a discrete selection of information from our universe. The selection process almost compels you to treat the book's subject matter as a consistent whole. That's one of the implicit concepts of a book—it has a beginning and an end, and it covers the subject matter fairly extensively. Yet a book creates an aspect of reality that does not exist, in the same way that, concentrating on a zebra's blackness, the light colored stripes would be phased out of the foreground of perception, temporarily giving the picture of a black zebra. I've tried to counter this problem of focusing on reality through a limited viewpoint with drawings, photos, poetry, and other peoples' points of view.

The other part of the analogy between books and zebras is painting the zebra all white—which is essentially what an author does with himself in a book. Authors have a whole spectrum of characteristics, and from these characteristics, using his language and a certain select viewpoint, he chooses a picture of himself. It is almost inevitably all white, because he has the time to select the thing he wants to use to impress others. My experience with authors is that the ones I know are quite different from the pictures they create of themselves in their books.

Salli wants a better explanation of this last point, without the zebras. Well, in a narrative book you try to transmit a segment of your personal experiences. How can the readers view their experience out of context from your background and your motives? They can't, and I wanted to get them in here. If, when you meet me, I'm like what you expect me to be, I get positive feedback that you "got" or "experienced" what I wrote about. If there were less of me in the book, or a "prettified" me, it would stand between us in communicating what I am talking about. A *Whole Earth Catalog* without the pages describing the production process and costs is a *Part Earth Catalog*.

Many authors, like Joyce, attempted to keep such a distortion process from affecting their work, but I question their success. In my own case, I have tried to write with all the blemishes and the nasty parts of my personality left in. I tried not to put them in here just for counterbalance or effect, but simply left them in wherever they appeared. Since most of this book was tape recorded, I have corrected the English, because there is a distinct difference between the way the eye hears and the way the ear hears, and a book, appropriately, should be written the way the eye hears. That's what I tried to do. I had hoped when I started that somebody who meets me after having read this book would have a fair understanding of what I am like.

LIBRARY OF CONGRESS
CATALOGING-IN-PUBLICATION DATA

Phillips, Michael, 1938–
The seven laws of money/Michael Phillips.
—1st Shambhala ed.
p.   cm. — (Shambhala pocket editions)
Originally published: [1st ed.]. Menlo Park, Calif.:
Word Wheel, [1974]. ISBN 0-87773-949-8
1. Money.   2. Finance,
Personal.   I. Title.   II. Series.
HG221.3.P5   1993   93-521
332'.024—dc20   CIP